a SAVOR THE SOUTH® *cookbook*

Gumbo

a SAVOR THE SOUTH® *cookbook*

Gumbo

DALE CURRY

The University of North Carolina Press CHAPEL HILL

The paper in this book meets the guidelines for permanence and durability of
the Committee on Production Guidelines for Book Longevity of the Council on
Library Resources. The University of North Carolina Press has been a member
of the Green Press Initiative since 2003.

Jacket illustration: bowl, © ksena32/Fotolia.com;
shrimp, © smuay/Fotolia.com; gumbo, © Jaimie Duplass/Fotolia.com

Library of Congress Cataloging-in-Publication Data
Curry, Dale.
Gumbo / by Dale Curry.
pages cm. — (Savor the South cookbooks)
Includes index.
ISBN 978-1-4696-2192-0 (cloth : alk. paper)
ISBN 978-1-4696-2268-2 (ebook)
1. Gumbo (Soup) 2. Cooking, American — Southern style. I. Title.
TX757.C8685 2015
641.81′3 — dc23   2014040784

Chef Emeril Lagasse's Gulf Coast Gumbo recipe courtesy of Emeril Lagasse,
© MSLO, Inc. All rights reserved.

To Matthew, Benjamin, Blair, and Allison

Contents

a SAVOR THE SOUTH® *cookbook*

Gumbo

Introduction

hen you live in New Orleans, your house becomes part home, part hotel because everyone you ever knew wants to come for a visit. There are many reasons for this—music, architecture, and the joie de vivre—but the big draw is the food, plain and simple.

Long ago, I established my plan for receiving these welcome guests: change the sheets and make a pot of gumbo. After that, they're on their own. Nobody's complained yet; I still have friends from childhood and college coming on a regular basis. The first thing they want when they get here is gumbo. While it's a regular on my menu, the dish is not a part of their weekly diets because they come from such locales as New York, Kansas, and California. Wherever they're from, though, their favorite version is seafood gumbo with crabs, shrimp, and oysters coming together in a single pot.

There is something about the smell of a simmering pot of gumbo that says "Louisiana." Its taste and aroma are unique. A change of atmosphere is noticeable when you drive south on the I-10 and smell the swamps and watch the egrets fly from one moss-covered cypress to another. Upon arrival, your first meal confirms a difference: You are in south Louisiana.

New Orleans is also known as the Big Easy, and one of a visitor's first experiences is sure to be a bowl of gumbo. It tingles your taste buds with spicy cayenne pepper and produces a taste you never forget. This pungent concoction of fresh seafood, meat, or poultry swimming in a dark liquid is the star of a cuisine that is unique in the world.

Called Creole in New Orleans and Cajun in southwest Louisiana, this cooking was born from several culinary sources—French, Spanish, German, African, Caribbean, and Native American—yet it is very different from each one. Despite its unusual character-istics, it is a regional American cuisine now known throughout the world. Of all the Creole-Cajun dishes, gumbo is the most rep-resentative. It is a soup made from a myriad of ingredients that must be well-seasoned. This book aims to show cooks how to do just that.

To understand the distinctions of Creole and Cajun cooking, it helps to know about the people who invented it. The first French and French Canadian settlers arrived in New Orleans in the early 1700s, followed shortly by ships carrying enslaved Africans through the Caribbean region. Germans settled forty miles up-river from New Orleans a few years later, and within forty years, Spanish had gained control of the colony. Meanwhile, interna-tional cooking styles began to merge, along with those of Native Americans. German farmers not only supplied the city with pro-duce and meat from the upriver parishes known as the German Coast; they also became the city's bread bakers. Their product was called French bread, but Germans had the monopoly on bak-ing it, and some of their bakeries still survive today. Then, in the late 1800s, Italians poured into New Orleans from Sicily, creating many of the city's early grocery stores and restaurants and hav-ing a major influence on the cuisine. To this day, neighborhood restaurants throughout New Orleans advertise "seafood and Ital-ian" as their fare.

In the mid-eighteenth century, a large group of descendants of French colonists, known as Acadians, were expelled by the British from Nova Scotia and surrounding areas, partly because they refused to take an oath against France. Following *Le Grand Dérangement*, or the Great Expulsion, many eventually found their way to southwest Louisiana and became known as Cajuns, a derivative of the word "Acadians." The deportation was me-morialized by Henry Wadsworth Longfellow in his epic poem "Evangeline."

New Orleans's earliest foreign settlers were French and French Canadian, whom the Spanish called "*Criollo*." The French trans-lation was "Creole," and the definition of Creole has evolved over the years. The Spanish first used the term to refer to the French-born in New Orleans. Later it was used for both French- and Spanish-born in Nouvelle Orléans. Those originating in the Old World were simply called French or Spanish. It was the Creoles themselves who first applied the term to persons of color. They used it to describe their property, much as we use the term "domestic" versus "imported" to specify local origin. "Creole" became an adjective for food and other things.

When the French arrived in New Orleans, a neighborhood was soon created on the Mississippi River overlooking a ninety-degree turn of the roaring river at its deepest point of 200 feet. It was called the *Vieux Carré* or French Quarter, and at its heart was the French Market. Early in the morning the market became the busiest place within hundreds of miles, bringing together farmers from upriver and fishermen from the bayous, Lake Pontchartrain, and the Gulf of Mexico. They bartered succulent oysters, fresh fish and shellfish, live poultry, and meat from farms west of the city. Produce that thrived in the warm, humid climate filled many of the stands. It wasn't long before restaurants opened alongside the market to feed the vendors as well as the travelers to the market. Some of the cooks in these restaurants were wives of vendors who helped establish a draw of visitors to New Orleans from far and wide to taste their unique style of cooking. The renowned Madame Elizabeth Begue and others created legendary dishes that attracted gourmets across the country as well as farmers across the street. In the late nineteenth century, her fifty-item Bohemian breakfast including wine cost $1.

Within the first decade after the city's founding in 1718, more than 5,000 enslaved Africans arrived in New Orleans. They brought to the port of New Orleans barrels of rice that became the most successful food crop to be cultivated in the new location, as well as okra, peas, beans, and yams. Much came from western Africa, while some was loaded up in the Caribbean Islands, where ships stopped for refreshment and supplies. Among the Caribbean contributions were a variety of spices. New arrivals in the 1780s broadened the scope of African influence, helping to build the French Quarter and farm the rice and sugar plantations along the Mississippi River. African cooking, and to a lesser degree

Caribbean, is a major thread in the quilt of southern cooking. Its influence contributed heavily to the staples of Louisiana cooking as we know it today in dishes such as gumbo, jambalaya, and red beans and rice.

France ceded Louisiana to Spain in 1762, and Spaniards brought in thousands of settlers, many of them from the Canary Islands, a Spanish archipelago off the coast of northwest Africa. They were known as the Islenos and settled on coastal properties as guardians of the territory from foreign intrusion. Many became fishermen, especially shrimpers, and one of their settlements downriver in St. Bernard Parish continues to preserve its cultural history today. The Islenos are known not only for their fishing and cooking but also for their intricate wood carvings of birds, ducks, and boats.

Spanish residents also influenced architecture in the French Quarter after fires in 1788 and 1794 destroyed most of the French colonial buildings. They were replaced with a Creole style, borrowed from African, French, Spanish, and Caribbean designs. The Cabildo on Jackson Square is the Quarter's most famous Spanish-designed building and is where the Louisiana Purchase was signed in 1803. The value placed by Europeans on growing and eating food became a way of life in Louisiana. The spirit of living to eat, rather than eating to live, and a relaxed and fun-loving lifestyle made New Orleans a center of entertainment and culinary excellence.

South Louisiana cooking was a secret among some of the world's gastronomes for more than 100 years before it was brought to the national and international forefront in the early 1980s in large part through the efforts of Cajun chef Paul Prudhomme. His popularity gave the cuisine the national label "Cajun" because he was from the southwest part of the state known as Cajun Country. The youngest child in a large family that fished, hunted, farmed, and cooked, Prudhomme learned to cook at the side of his mother and used his talents to become executive chef of Commander's Palace and to create his own now-famous restaurant, K-Paul's Louisiana Kitchen, and a spice company that supplies restaurants and stores all over the world.

While the Cajun rage flourished, New Orleans cooking was for the most part Creole. Many words have been written to explain the difference, but the simplest version is that Cajun is country-style and more like home cooking while Creole is fancier with French sauces and techniques. Cajuns are known for their hunting and fishing abilities as well as their talent for turning their catch into delectable meals. And they are more likely to serve it on a kitchen table than on a white tablecloth. Creoles, with their flair for savoring and serving food, retained a formality that focused on mealtime and entertaining. Both populations were Roman Catholic and were influenced by religious restrictions on eating meat on certain days, particularly during Lent, adding to the popularity of the abundant seafood. Although Friday abstinence of meat has been relaxed in the church, hundreds of seafood restaurants have waiting lines on Fridays.

South Louisiana has held on to lots of traditional customs, whether casual or formal, in many aspects of life. For example, New Orleans is the nation's only city still using electric streetcars for major public transportation. Old buildings are treasured, and antique furnishings preferred. Some restaurants in New Orleans serve exactly the same dishes they were serving fifty or more years ago, and the crowds are still coming. That's not to say that cutting-edge chefs don't abound; they certainly do. This cookbook features recipes by some of the top James Beard Award–winning chefs from the Crescent City. These chefs often embellish 100-year-old dishes with new ideas, yet their menus still offer traditional gumbos, étouffées, and court bouillons.

When native New Orleanians go to the market or grocery store, they often say they are "making groceries." The expression comes from the French term *faire son marche*, "to do one's market shopping"; *faire* means either "to do" or "to make."

In 1803, the United States purchased the Louisiana territory from France, establishing fifteen states, including Louisiana. Some of us who have moved to south Louisiana from other states over the years have adopted Cajun and Creole cooking because it is so contagious. I still cook my Tennessee-Mississippi favorites, but most of my cooking is strongly Cajun-Creole style. Although there are regional differences in cuisine throughout the South, it is hard to find a restaurant featuring what is often referred to as "southern cooking" in New Orleans. In the northern part of Louisiana, cooking styles are more like those of other southern states than southern Louisiana styles. Nevertheless, a very spicy version of fried chicken that originated in greater New Orleans and went international is wildly popular. Until recently, barbecue, another southern favorite, was almost nonexistent in New Orleans. Instead, backyard gatherings often feature boiling shellfish, particularly crawfish. Lately, a few barbecue restaurants have opened, and chefs of all kinds are tinkering with pulled pork in a myriad of dishes.

New Orleans cooks generally have survived the era of cooking with canned soup, and the fast-food bombardment of America, to favor grandmothers' recipes. This is true even in their choices of dining out. It would be rare for me to go to a hamburger chain when I could have a po'boy of crisp French bread loaded with freshly fried oysters any place in the city.

Men and women alike do the cooking in south Louisiana, and men are generally in charge of backyard boils, where everything is cooked in one huge pot that will hold twenty-five or more pounds of crawfish, plus potatoes, corn, artichokes, onions, garlic, and more. Most love a challenge and take to deep-frying turkeys. Some are brave enough to take on turducken, which entails deboning and stuffing a chicken inside a duck inside a turkey. Each fowl is stuffed with a different kind of dressing, such as shrimp dressing or oyster dressing. Louisianans love to hunt, fish, and crab, and they often cook at their camps in the wetlands. Shucking bags of oysters and smoking chickens atop beer cans are other favorite pastimes. The long afternoons of cooking are almost as much fun as the eating. And many a playful argument ensues over the right way to boil crawfish. In Louisiana, if you're not cooking, you're eating, and if you're eating lunch, you're probably talking about what you'll be having for dinner.

My love of gumbo goes back to childhood when my mother and I took exciting train trips from Memphis to New Orleans to visit my grandmother, who lived just outside the city. An uncle would meet us at the train station, and before long we were sitting at my grandmother's table feasting on shrimp-and-okra gumbo. That's river shrimp, the little ones that came from the Mississippi River before pollution stopped the practice of shrimping in the giant waterway. At my aunt's house, we ate crawfish bisque, and at Middendorf's, a favorite restaurant in the swamps where Lakes Pontchartrain and Maurepas meet, we ordered great piles of boiled crabs. We are still regulars at that eighty-year-old restaurant.

As a little girl, I once spent a frantic night at my grandmother's when I went into the kitchen for a drink of water, turned on the light, and found a floor covered in live crabs walking sideways. They had worked their way out of a tin washtub in which they were being kept to be cooked the next day. I ran through the house, screaming, and woke everybody up. They ran around grabbing crabs this way and that, throwing them into the bin, and this time covering them up securely. Scared out of my wits though I was, it didn't stop me from eating my fill of the spicy boiled crabs and gumbo she prepared the next day.

Some of the dishes I marveled over were unique to south Louisiana, and so different from the southern cooking I was accustomed to. New Orleans was like a foreign country, and I jumped at the chance to move here as a young adult. Over the years, I have introduced many friends, as well as my husband, to picking crabs, peeling crawfish, slurping oysters, and making a roux. It was so much fun that it turned me, a news reporter, into a food writer, and there I have been for the last thirty years.

In the first part of this cookbook, I present all of the gumbos that I know how to cook. There may be other versions, and mixing and matching ingredients is always possible. You can really put any meat, fish, or fowl into a gumbo as long as you build a good seasoning base around it. I begin with three special gumbos, contributed by outstanding chefs who take their talents to the limit everyday with old and new versions of Cajun-Creole cooking, including gumbos.

The first part also features a number of versions of jambalaya, another Louisiana favorite that's a casual, fun food that can be at the center of any party. I've included a few celebrity chefs' recipes here as well as many of my own.

Like gumbo, many other Louisiana dishes represent a melting pot of nations. The culinary traditions indigenous to the area combine Native American, French, Spanish, African, Caribbean, Italian, and German. And through this many-colored mixture, the region, like a gumbo, gains its singular identity.

The second part of the book offers an extra portion of Louisiana favorites. The word "lagniappe" (LAN-yap) could describe a gift basket given to someone you're entertaining in New Orleans. It might be the thirteenth doughnut thrown in for free when you buy a dozen. In this case, it is all about the regional dishes prepared in New Orleans and across the southern part of Louisiana, in addition—a bonus of sorts—to gumbo and jambalaya.

Gumbo

Gumbo is the essence of Creole and Cajun cooking, the mandatory dish on every restaurant menu and the heart of home cooking. It showcases the best indigenous shellfish as well as local sausages, poultry, wild game, and spices. It originated in Louisiana in the eighteenth century and derives its name from either the Bantu word for okra (*gombo*) or the Choctaw word for filé (*kombo*). Both okra and filé, which is ground sassafras leaves used by Native Americans, serve as thickeners for gumbo, along with the roux, a base of flour browned in oil. The most common thickener is the roux, which is similar to gravy. The extent to which it is browned determines the color of the gumbo. Local cooks often take it to a dark-brown color that gives the finished product a deep and robust flavor. Traditionally, onions, celery, and bell pepper (known as the trinity of local cooking) plus garlic are sizzled in the roux, and stock is added to make a soup. Ingredients ranging from shellfish to poultry to wild game create the type and taste of the gumbo. Seasonings such as cayenne pepper, thyme, and bay leaf alter the flavor of the dish to please the cook, and the gumbo is served in bowls over rice.

The most distinctive styles of gumbo are Creole (New Orleans) and Cajun (southwestern Louisiana). Creole uses tomatoes, and Cajun does not. Therefore, one is brown and the other is a reddish brown. Creole gumbo tends to have a thinner base, while a Cajun gumbo is heartier, darker and sometimes thicker, and is more apt to use game such as wild ducks. In south Louisiana, gumbos are served on all tables, rich or poor, and in most restaurants, upscale or otherwise.

In New Orleans's early days, a gumbo was likely served as the first course of a meal. Today, given our fast-paced lives, a gumbo usually counts as the entrée on home tables. Restaurants are more likely to follow the old-school style with gumbo as an appetizer.

I've learned from decades of living in this seductive city that there are as many gumbos as there are cooks. I, for one, am forever changing my recipes a bit here and a bit there. My guests prefer seafood gumbo, my family likes chicken and andouille gumbo, and I personally believe you can't beat a good duck gumbo. I once tasted a gumbo by a well-known visiting chef who garnished his gumbo with shrimp heads. Aghast, I could only guess that he confused sucking crawfish heads, a tasty rite of eating boiled crawfish, with serving a seafood gumbo. He was competing in a gumbo contest, which, alas, he lost. (I was a judge!)

With this in mind, there are several generally accepted rules for cooking gumbo, although they are probably violated as often as not:

* Never put filé in a gumbo while it is cooking. It should be added only after cooking. Don't warm up gumbo that has filé in it or it may be ropey. It is best to pass the filé at the table and add to bowls individually.
* Sauté okra separately before adding it to the gumbo. Cooking evaporates the liquid that causes the okra—and gumbo—to be slimy.
* Brown meats before adding them to gumbo. This creates flavor.
* Long-grain white rice is commonly preferred with gumbo.

✳ Always season a gumbo well. The seasoning comes from the vegetables—onion, bell pepper, celery, and garlic—added at the beginning, as well as plentiful herbs and pepper.

The 1901 edition of *The Picayune's Creole Cook Book* included ten recipes for gumbo featuring ingredients ranging from squirrel to cabbage. Others included chicken, ham, oysters, crabs, and shrimp. All were considered "Creole," which was described as "an original conception, a something *sui generis* in cooking, peculiar to this ancient Creole city alone, and to the manner born." Its recipes were "gathered with care from the best Creole housekeepers of New Orleans . . . handed down from generation to generation."

There is no doubt that Native Americans, slave traders, and enslaved Africans played a major role in gumbo's creation. A key ingredient, ground sassafras leaves, or filé, was introduced by Native Americans, who used the sassafras plant for medicinal purposes. In the late 1800s, Choctaw Indians, who dried the tender leaves, ground them into a fine powder, and then passed the powder through a hair sieve, supplied the New Orleans market from a reservation on Bayou Lacombe on the north shore of Lake Pontchartrain.

During the era of slave trading, okra was introduced to New Orleans by Africans, who, most food experts believe, brought the plant to southern plantations via the Caribbean. It was called *gombo* or *kingombo* in Bantu languages and was either boiled, fried, steamed, or pickled and served as both a thickener and a tasty ingredient that pairs well with seafood in gumbos.

Today, the meaning of "gumbo" goes beyond the culinary. Most any mixture might be called a gumbo—a political gumbo, a breed of dog, a fashion craze. It is a popular name for animals; one in particular was a St. Bernard and mascot of the New Orleans Saints in its early years.

Of all the dishes served in the melting pot, or gumbo, that is south Louisiana, this pungent, one-pot dish has become synonymous with the territory. Say "New Orleans," and we think "food" or we think "gumbo."

Jambalaya

I have included a few jambalaya recipes in this book. Rice is at the heart of many south Louisiana dishes, none more so than jambalaya. While gumbo is served over rice, jambalaya is an entrée made of rice fused with meats and seafood. It is a one-pot dish, usually spicy, or served with hot sauce on the side. Like gumbo, the Creole version is likely to contain tomatoes while the Cajun variation is not. Unlike gumbo, jambalaya does not contain a roux. Shrimp is the most common ingredient in Creole jambalaya, usually along with chicken and/or smoked link sausage. Cajun jambalaya is as likely to include crawfish or alligator in addition to shrimp and sausage.

Jambalaya is similar to the Spanish paella and believed to have been influenced by the Spanish during Spain's possession of Louisiana in the late eighteenth century. Instead of mussels and clams, Louisiana's jambalaya sported shrimp, oysters, and crabs. The state's abundant rice crop made it a natural.

Jambalaya is a casually served and filling dish, a favorite at football parties and outdoor gatherings. In the old days, jambalaya was a depository for leftovers. It is rarely served in upscale restaurants but is popular in casual neighborhood restaurants. It is sometimes used as a stuffing for poultry. Many Thanksgiving turkeys are stuffed with a rice dressing similar to jambalaya. A stunning dish is a jambalaya-stuffed quail served in a dark gumbo.

Theories abound as to the origins of the term "jambalaya." It is commonly believed to have gotten its name from the French word *jambon*, meaning ham, another ingredient that works well in the dish. But modern cooks tend to prefer sausages to ham in jambalaya, probably because of their spiciness and the high quality of sausages in the region. Some historians argue that the term is derived from the Provençal word "jambalaia," dating to 1837, or an Arabic word for which I have no exact translation, but both indicating "mixture." The term is also said to have referred to a Native American cereal of wild rice; a use for rice brought to the Gulf Coast from Africa, where the word for rice is variously "ya," "aya," or "yaya"; a version of Hopping John carried from North Carolina to Louisiana via Mobile, Alabama, by an enslaved African who wrote a cookbook on southern cooking and another Mobile church-published cookbook in 1881. Since no one knows for sure where the word comes from, I think it best to say the dish belongs to all and still lives at the heart of south Louisiana cooking.

One of my daughter's favorite dish was jambalaya, and I made it for every occasion involving her. When she came home from college, jambalaya was always on the stove. She liked it with whole pieces of chicken, browned first and cooked in the jambalaya, and that was how I made it for many years. Lately, I have used a rotisserie chicken from the store, deboned it, and chopped up the pieces. It can be as easy as you make it and still be delicious. Most people like it spicy and washed down with cold beer.

Gonzales, a town along the Airline Highway between New Orleans and Baton Rouge, is known as the Jambalaya Capitol of the World. Every year in late spring, cooks get out their black iron cauldrons and cook the dish they are famous for, always competing to be the best cook at the Gonzales Jambalaya Festival. Fun, food, music, and activities go on for four days with jambalaya served all day, everyday.

Jambalaya owes much of it renown to country music. It became famous with the song "Jambalaya (on the Bayou)," released by Hank Williams in the 1950s.

Lagniappe

The word "lagniappe," meaning "a little something extra," is commonly used in New Orleans. It might refer to an unexpected gift or an extra bedtime story for a child. In this case, it is extra recipes in addition to the gumbos and jambalayas. "Lagniappe" is the French term for a concept brought to New Orleans by the Spanish, at the time applied to the practice of a store owner offering a customer an extra number or portion of something he or she was purchasing. Just as gumbo and jambalaya are unique to south Louisiana, so are many other dishes that draw hundreds of thousands of people to the city annually. Many say they come to eat.

No wonder that quite a few dishes and drinks were invented in New Orleans. Gumbo and jambalaya were, of course, two of them. They were born in the bayous and crafted by the working hands of fishermen's wives, cooks in the kitchens of stately homes, and men, women, and children who grew up cooking the copious ingredients surrounding them.

Then came the restaurants, the laboratories for creative chefs and restaurateurs.

In the 1950s, when most bananas imported to the United States came through the Port of New Orleans. Owen Brennan Sr., the founder of Brennan's restaurant, a New Orleans institution, challenged his chef, Paul Blangé, to find a new way to use the plentiful fruit. Blangé created Bananas Foster, named for a friend, Richard Foster, a frequent diner at Brennan's and vice chairman of the city's vice committee in charge of cleaning up the French Quarter. Bananas are cooked in a chafing dish with banana liqueur and rum, flamed, and served over vanilla ice cream.

Antoine's restaurant, which opened in 1840 and is New Orleans's oldest restaurant, created eggs Sardou for a dinner that Antoine Alciatore, the restaurant's founder, hosted for the French playwright Victorien Sardou. Antoine's also invented oysters Rockefeller, a succulent dish of oysters baked on the half shell that has been copied by many others. Surprisingly, most chefs use spinach in the sauce that blankets the oysters, but Antoine's secret recipe does not include it. Antoine's topping is green but is made of other green vegetables, likely green onions, celery, bell pepper, basil, and parsley. Its striking anise flavor comes from Herbsaint, a New Orleans–invented liqueur that serves as a substitute for the illegal absinthe, which has now been legalized in some areas, including New Orleans.

Oysters Bienville, a dish also featuring oysters baked on the half shell and created at one of the city's oldest restaurants, Arnaud's, is the namesake of the founder of New Orleans, Jean Baptiste le Moyne, Sieur de Bienville. Arnaud's is located on Bienville Street in the French Quarter. The original owner, Leon Bertrand Arnaud Casenave, well-known as Count Arnaud, created the dish with the help of his chefs.

The Ramos Gin Fizz, a favorite of Louisiana governor Huey Long, was created by Henry C. Ramos, a bar owner who arrived in New Orleans in 1888. It was served and trademarked at the Roosevelt Hotel's Sazerac Bar. It contains orange flower water, sweet gin, and milk.

The po'boy, or poor boy, a lunch staple in New Orleans, was the brainy idea of two kindly sandwich shop owners who took pity on the starving streetcar drivers during a strike in the 1920s. They handed out free sandwiches consisting of a slice of meat between two pieces of New Orleans's wonderful French bread, keeping the "poor boys" alive. The benevolent shop owners were Bennie and Clovis Martin, who at one time had been streetcar conductors themselves. Most of the bakeries at the time were owned by German immigrants, and some of those still exist today; one of them, Gendusa's, began making the long loaves of French bread to accommodate the sandwiches. Today, po'boys are among the most popular dishes in New Orleans. The sandwiches are made with many different kinds of seafood, meat, cheese, and vegetables, but the most popular fillings are oysters, shrimp, and roast beef with gravy. Most locals like them "dressed," meaning they are outfitted with lettuce and tomato.

The muffuletta, a version of an Italian sandwich originating in Sicily, was first served at Central Grocery in the French Quarter. The kind served in New Orleans consists of a round loaf of Italian bread loaded with imported cheeses and meats, topped with the magic of the sandwich—a generous portion of olive salad, containing a variety of imported olives.

The most famous drink associated with New Orleans is the Hurricane, invented at Pat O'Brien's during World War II by Charlie Cantrell, a co-owner, when rum was plentiful and other spirits were not. It is made of rum and fruit juices, including passion fruit, and has its own special glass, shaped like a hurricane lamp and sold by the tens of thousands each year at the French Quarter bar.

Before the Hurricane came the Sazerac cocktail, a potent drink containing Herbsaint, two kinds of bitters, and rye whiskey. Invented in 1850 at a New Orleans coffee house, it was made of Sazerac-de-Forge, a French cognac, and Peychaud's bitters, which were created in New Orleans. The Roosevelt Hotel's Sazerac Bar, one of the most popular bars in New Orleans, is named after the drink. Today's now-famous recipe was created in 1870 when bartender Leon Lamothe added absinthe to it and replaced the cognac with American rye whiskey. Sazerac rye whiskey and Peychaud Bitters are now distilled in Kentucky by a company owned by the historic Sazerac Company of New Orleans.

Not invented in New Orleans but of major importance to the city's tourists and locals are French beignets, served up by the thousands each day by two long-established coffeehouses, Café du Monde and Morning Call. I once interviewed Julia Child over coffee and beignets at the original mid-eighteenth-century French Market coffee stand and asked what she thought of the beignets. In her usual forthright manner, she replied, "A beignet is a beignet." So true, as New Orleans's version is exactly the same as France's. Café du Monde is open 24/7 and closes only on Christmas and when the occasional hurricane hits. Its beignets are served lavishly covered in powdered sugar, while the Morning Call offers the powdered sugar in shakers on the side.

All of which point to the culture that created a cuisine known throughout the world. Of all the Creole-Cajun dishes, gumbo is most representative. While many commonly call for ingredients that are indigenous to Louisiana, it can be made anywhere. I know. I've made it in Topeka, Kansas. I've made it in Los Angeles. If you have access to chicken and smoked sausage, you've got a gumbo. The same goes for jambalaya. If you've got rice, sausage, and chicken, you're in luck. Just make sure it's well-seasoned.

You can call it peasant food. You can deem it fit for gourmets. Like America, Cajun-Creole cuisine is a mix from many nationalities. The United States is not known for just one cuisine. Rather, our culinary repertoire is made up of regional cuisines, among which Cajun-Creole is the best known. It gathers people together to celebrate their heritage. More than 400 Louisiana festivals occur each year, which makes it easy to see why Louisiana is often called the Festival Capital of America. We celebrate just about every crop harvested, every indigenous dish, and every type of music played here. There are several gumbo festivals in different locations, the jambalaya festival in Gonzales, the strawberry festival in Ponchatoula, and the tomato festival in Chalmette. There is the crawfish festival in Breaux Bridge, the catfish festival in Washington Parish, and the andouille festival in LaPlace, ninety miles upriver from New Orleans and near the German Coast. Food stands for family and comfort, and food is what brings them together.

When people born and raised here decide to move away (and it is rare and painful), they often continue to celebrate Mardi Gras and Jazz Fest wherever they live. How do they do it? They have king cakes shipped in from New Orleans bakeries, they cook pots of gumbo and jambalaya, and they put on jazz or zydeco music. This is what a celebration tastes like.

Some Terms You Should Know

The following are terms you should know for using this cookbook:

Andouille: a lean, highly flavorful smoked sausage made of pork butt.

Boudin: a rice sausage popular in southwest Louisiana and often eaten for breakfast.

Chaurice: a spicy Creole pork sausage similar to chorizo, a Spanish sausage.

Creole seasoning: an all-in-one, sprinkle-on seasoning usually containing salt, cayenne pepper, paprika, black pepper, chili powder, garlic, and other spices.

Filé powder: ground sassafras leaves used for thickening and seasoning gumbos, introduced by Choctaw Indians, who used the powder for medicinal purposes in tonics and teas.

Gumbo crabs: small crabs commonly cleaned and frozen for use in gumbos.

Tasso: heavily seasoned smoked pieces of pork butt used for seasoning.

Gumbo

There is something about the smell of a
simmering pot of gumbo that says "Louisiana."
Its taste and aroma are truly unique.

Roux

For most gumbos, you first need to make a roux, which gives gumbo flavor, color, and thickness. A roux is simply flour browned in oil, and the amount of each ingredient you use depends on the quantity you are cooking and the thickness you desire. The following recipe will provide enough roux for a gumbo to serve about six people.

MAKES ABOUT 1 CUP

½ cup vegetable oil
½ cup all-purpose flour

Heat the oil in a large, heavy pot over high heat; add the flour and stir constantly until the mixture begins to brown. Reduce the heat to medium or medium-low and cook, stirring constantly, until the roux is medium-brown, or the color of peanut butter or milk chocolate.

If you prefer a darker gumbo, continue browning until the roux turns a dark-chocolate color. The darker the roux, the thinner the gumbo will be. Do not burn the roux, or it will ruin the taste of the gumbo. If it smells burnt, it has cooked too long. Most gumbos are tasty and slightly thick when the roux is the color of milk chocolate.

Seafood Stock

A seafood stock is simple. It doesn't cook long and can be made from peelings from the seafood you are using in a gumbo or other dish. The heads of shrimp and crawfish are particularly important because they contain a tasty fat that adds flavor to your dish.

MAKES 5 CUPS

1½ pounds shells from shrimp, crawfish, or crabs

Place shells in a medium pot and cover with cold water. Bring to a boil. Cover, reduce heat to medium-low and simmer for 30 minutes. Strain.

Poultry Stock

Poultry stock can be used to flavor chicken, duck, turkey, quail, and sometimes even seafood soups and gumbos. You can make this with fresh chicken parts or a leftover carcass after cooking and carving.

MAKES 8 CUPS

3 pounds chicken, turkey, or duck bones (including the
   carcass or bony parts such as necks and backs)
1 large onion, peeled and quartered
2 celery stalks, halved
2 carrots, quartered
½ tablespoon black peppercorns
2 large garlic cloves, halved
10 cups cold water

Place all the ingredients in a 6-quart pot. Bring to a boil. Reduce the heat to medium-low, cover the pot with the lid askew, and simmer for 2½ hours. When cool enough to handle, strain. Cool completely and skim the fat from the top. If making ahead, chill in the refrigerator and skim off the solid fat.

Rice

There is no need to look for shortcuts in cooking rice. There is nothing easier than simmering enriched rice. For gumbos and jambalayas, I prefer long grain or extra long grain.

MAKES 6–8 SERVINGS

2 cups water
2 cups enriched long-grain rice
½ teaspoon salt

In a small pot with a cover, bring the water to a boil. Add the rice and salt. Reduce the heat, cover, and simmer on the lowest heat until the water is absorbed, about 20 minutes. No stirring is necessary.

Creole Seasoning

Before Paul Prudhomme became Louisiana's star chef in the 1980s, he traveled to different parts of the country working in restaurants, always carrying a mixture of his favorite seasonings with him to spice up the food and make it taste like home. Since that time, he and a dozen others have created spice mixes that can be found in grocery stores from here to Asia. Creole seasoning is as common as salt in a south Louisiana recipe. Many local brands such as Prudhomme's, Tony Chachere's, Rex, and Zatarain's are widely used, but this is easy to make.

MAKES 2 ½ OUNCES

---

2 tablespoons salt

2 teaspoons cayenne pepper

4 teaspoons freshly ground black pepper

4 teaspoons garlic powder

4 teaspoons paprika, sweet or hot, or to taste

4 teaspoons celery salt

2 teaspoons chili powder

Whisk together all the ingredients in a medium bowl. Store in a cleaned 2½-ounce spice bottle. The seasoning will keep its strength for several months.

PREPARING CRABS

Blue crabs, the same species for which Maryland is known, are widely available in south Louisiana. The lakes and bayous are filled with them, and crabbing is sport for many, including children. Seafood stores sell them live as well as boiled and highly seasoned. They also stock frozen gumbo crabs, selected for their small size. These are perfect for gumbo because they are already cleaned and ready to drop in a gumbo.

If using frozen crabs, thaw and wipe them clean and break them in two. They go into a gumbo in the early stages of cooking because they are a great source of flavor. Diners often like to pick them up and suck the juices and whatever meat is left out of them. If you want shelled lump crabmeat in a gumbo, it must be added at the end of cooking. It can be purchased by the pint, cooked and cleaned. It should be checked over for any shell fragments remaining.

To use live crabs, place them in a pot of boiling water for 1 minute, just long enough to kill them. When cool enough to handle, pull the backs off and clean out all but the yellow fat in the center of the crabs. Remove the eyes and "dead man's fingers," or lungs, across the top of each side. Break the crabs in two, and they are ready to go in a gumbo.

Some cooks use boiled and seasoned crabs in gumbo. The only drawback is that wonderful crab flavor comes from cooking the raw crab in the gumbo. It is, however, preferable to using canned crab or no crab at all in a seafood gumbo.

Chef Emeril Lagasse's
Gulf Coast Gumbo

Chef Emeril and I go back to 1987 when the Association of Food Journalists (AFJ) held its annual conference in New Orleans. He was executive chef at Commander's Palace and prepared a lovely luncheon for 110 food writers from all over the country and beyond. I was chairman of the conference, and the newspaper I worked for, the Times-Picayune, *hosted the luncheon. He later became world-famous, owning restaurants in several locations, including three in New Orleans—Emeril's, NOLA, and Emeril's Delmonico. He cooked at two later AFJ conferences, one in Orlando and another in New Orleans. He is known for his many philanthropic endeavors to help young people, including major funding of Café Reconcile, a restaurant in New Orleans training at-risk youth in restaurant careers. Among the many awards Lagasse has won is the 2013 James Beard Humanitarian of the Year Award.*

Of this recipe, the chef says, "Some of the world's best seafood comes from the Gulf Coast, so I highly recommend using fresh Gulf seafood whenever possible."

MAKES 8 SERVINGS

- 1 cup vegetable oil
- 1½ cups all-purpose flour
- 2½ cups chopped onion
- 1½ cups chopped celery
- 1½ cups chopped green bell pepper
- 3 tablespoons chopped garlic
- 1 teaspoon Emeril's Original Essence or other Creole seasoning
- 1½ teaspoons salt
- 1 teaspoon freshly ground black pepper
- ½ teaspoon cayenne pepper
- 2 bay leaves

1 teaspoon dried thyme

1 teaspoon dried oregano

1 pound smoked sausage, cut into ½-inch-thick rounds

1 pound gumbo crabs, halved (see Note)

10 cups shrimp stock or water

1 pound cooked Louisiana crawfish tails, with any fat

1 pound peeled and deveined Gulf shrimp

½ cup chopped green onions, plus more for serving

¼ cup chopped fresh parsley leaves, plus more for serving

Steamed white rice, for serving

Heat a large Dutch oven or heavy-bottomed soup pot over high heat for 1 minute. Carefully add the oil and then whisk in the flour. Reduce the heat to medium-high and stir the flour constantly, scraping every bit of the pan bottom, until the roux is evenly browned and the color of dark peanut butter, about 15 minutes. If the flour begins to color too fast, reduce the heat to medium. It is important to watch the roux and cook carefully to avoid burning it. Once the desired color is reached, add the onion, celery, bell pepper, garlic, Essence, salt, pepper, cayenne, bay leaves, thyme, oregano, and sausage. Continue to cook 5–7 minutes longer, or until the vegetables have softened.

Add the crabs and stock to the Dutch oven and bring to a boil. Reduce the heat to a steady simmer and cook until the flavors have come together and the sauce is velvety and smooth, about 2 hours, adding additional stock or water if the gumbo becomes too thick during cooking. The thickness of a gumbo is a matter of personal taste. Some folks like a very thick gumbo, while others prefer a thin, brothy gumbo. Add the amount of liquid to suit your preference.

When the gumbo is flavorful and just the right thickness, stir in the crawfish and shrimp and cook just until the shrimp are cooked through, 2–3 minutes longer. Stir in the green onions and parsley. Taste and adjust the seasoning, if necessary.

Serve the gumbo over bowls of steamed rice with additional chopped parsley and green onions as desired.

NOTE ✳ Gumbo crabs are blue crabs that are not graded number 1, simply because they may not be as heavy/full of crabmeat as number 1–graded crabs. They are kept aside and sold as gumbo crabs for folks to flavor soups and stews, such as this gumbo. You can often find them in the freezer section of grocery stores in Louisiana, but if you cannot find them where you live, you can simply substitute 2 regular blue crabs, if desired.

Chef Donald Link's Chicken, Shrimp, and Tasso Gumbo

Chef Donald Link is one of New Orleans's premier chefs, having grown up to the west of the city, in Cajun Country, and bringing his talents to a number of the Crescent City's top restaurants. In 2007, he was named the James Beard Best Chef South. Since opening his first restaurant, Herbsaint, with acclaimed chef Susan Spicer, he has opened the popular Cochon, Cochon Butcher, and Peche restaurants and Calcasieu, a private-event facility.

About this recipe, he says, "Growing up in Southwest Louisiana, we had chicken and sausage gumbo or seafood gumbo; it was rare to find a combination. I think the three ingredients in this recipe really complement each other. Sausage can be a bit overpowering for shrimp, but the tasso keeps all the ingredients on an even playing field. I will generally make my roux somewhat lighter for gumbos with seafood present because it helps that flavor stand out. If you have the time, I suggest making a shrimp stock with the shells from the shrimp and using half chicken, half shrimp stock."

MAKES 6–8 SERVINGS

4 boneless chicken thighs, cut into 2-inches pieces
    with the skin on
2 teaspoons kosher salt
1/2 teaspoon paprika
1/2 teaspoon freshly ground black pepper
1 1/2 cups vegetable oil
2 1/4 cups all-purpose flour, divided
1 pound diced tasso
1 medium onion, small diced
2 poblano peppers, small diced
1 small jalapeño, small diced
3 celery stalks, diced
4 garlic cloves, minced

2–3 teaspoons kosher salt (add 2, taste, and add the other
   if needed)

1½ teaspoons freshly ground black pepper

1 teaspoon cayenne pepper

1 teaspoon paprika

1 teaspoon dried thyme

1 teaspoon filé powder

6 bay leaves

1 gallon chicken stock (or half shrimp stock and half
   chicken stock)

1 pound peeled Louisiana shrimp

Season the chicken with the salt, paprika, and pepper.

Heat the oil in a 2-gallon heavy-bottomed pot to medium-high heat; the oil should gently sizzle when it is ready.

Coat the chicken with ½ cup of the flour and fry on both sides in the oil until light golden brown, then remove to a paper towel. It does not have to be cooked through at this point. Add any excess flour from seasoning the chicken to the remaining flour and add it to the oil. Stir over medium heat for about 40 minutes, or until the roux turns a deep reddish brown, but not too dark.

After the roux reaches the right color, add the tasso, the vegetables, and all the spices (reserving that little bit of salt, because some tasso is spicier than others) and cook for about 4 minutes.

Whisk in the stock and bring to a simmer, being sure to stir the bottom of the pot as the gumbo comes to a simmer so it doesn't stick. Simmer for about 30 minutes while skimming all the fat that rises to the surface.

Add the cooked chicken and shrimp at this point and simmer for another 45 minutes, still skimming any fat that floats to the top.

Serve immediately or the next day with some steamed rice and a side of creamy potato salad. Chef Link says, "I like to dip my potato salad in the gumbo."

Chef Leah Chase's Creole Gumbo

Leah Chase is the grande dame of Creole cooking in New Orleans. In her nineties, she continues to command the kitchen of Dooky Chase Restaurant, an institution in the city for more than sixty years and a location where prominent civil rights leaders gathered when whites-only restaurants were the norm. She is the recipient of many national and local awards for her leadership in community affairs and her culinary talents. She has served two acting U.S. presidents in her restaurant. On one visit to New Orleans, President Obama ate lunch there, but the next time he was in town, his schedule was too tight to visit her. Instead, an aide came to the restaurant and picked up gumbo, fried chicken, jambalaya, and shrimp Creole for the president to eat on the plane. Chase also served dinner to President George W. Bush at her restaurant. Another time, the president invited her to have dinner with him at Commander's Palace. After dinner, he asked if she would fix breakfast the following morning. Although her restaurant is not open for breakfast, she said, "You don't turn down a president." So the next morning, President Bush dined at her restaurant, where she prepared grits, shrimp, quail, and catfish. The president of Mexico and the prime minister of Canada were there, too. This is a version of her legendary gumbo.

MAKES 8–10 SERVINGS

½ pound chaurice, cut into bite-size pieces

½ pound smoked sausage, cut into bite-size pieces

½ pound beef stew meat

½ pound chicken gizzards, chopped

1 pound gumbo crabs

½ cup vegetable oil

½ cup all-purpose flour

2 large onions, chopped

3 quarts water, or more as desired

8 chicken wings, cut at joints and tips discarded
½ pound smoked ham, cut into ½-inch pieces
1 tablespoon paprika
1 teaspoon dried thyme
1 teaspoon salt
3 garlic cloves, minced
1 pound medium shrimp, peeled and deveined
2 dozen shucked oysters with their liquor
¼ cup chopped fresh flat-leaf parsley
1 tablespoon filé powder
Cooked long-grain white rice, for serving

Place the sausages, beef, gizzards, and crabs in a large, heavy pot. Cover and cook over medium heat for 30 minutes, stirring occasionally. You won't need extra fat, as the meat will render enough for cooking.

While the meats are cooking, make a roux: heat the oil in a skillet, add the flour, and stir constantly over medium heat until the roux is smooth and dark-brown in color. Add the onions and cook over low heat until soft. Empty the contents of the skillet into the pot holding the meat, mixing well. Slowly stir in the water and bring it to a boil. Add the chicken wings, ham, paprika, thyme, salt, and garlic, stir gently, and turn down the heat; cover and simmer for 45 minutes. If you prefer a thinner gumbo, add more water now.

Add the shrimp and oysters and cook several more minutes — watch for the shrimp to turn just pink and the oysters to curl — any more than that, and they will become tough. Remove the pot from the heat, stir in the parsley and filé powder, and enjoy in bowls over hot rice.

Creole Seafood Gumbo

This gumbo is the essence of Louisiana. In one pot, it combines the state's finest specimens of shellfish with local produce and spices. It is the dish the world comes to New Orleans to eat. When you make it from scratch (peeling shrimp, making stock) it takes a while to prepare, and it is not inexpensive, but when you do make the effort, you have a pot to be proud of and a dish to please.

MAKES 6–8 SERVINGS

6 medium blue crabs or frozen gumbo crabs, thawed

2½ pounds shrimp in shells with heads

2 dozen medium-to-large shucked oysters with their liquor

1 cup plus 1 tablespoon canola or other vegetable oil, divided

2 cups sliced okra, fresh or frozen and thawed

1 cup all-purpose flour

1 large onion, chopped

1 bunch green onions, chopped, white and green parts separated

1 green bell pepper, chopped

2 celery stalks, chopped

4 large garlic cloves, minced

2 large fresh tomatoes in season, peeled and chopped, or 1 (16-ounce) canned diced tomatoes with juice

3 bay leaves

1 teaspoon Italian seasoning

Salt, freshly ground black pepper, and Creole seasoning, to taste

¼ cup minced flat-leaf parsley

Cooked long-grain white rice, for serving

Prepare the crabs as described in "Preparing Crabs," page 23.

De-head, peel, and devein the shrimp, placing the heads and shells in a medium pot. Add enough water to cover the shells by at least 2 inches and bring to a boil. Cover, reduce the heat to low, and simmer for 30 minutes. When slightly cooled, strain the stock into a large measuring cup and discard the shells.

Strain the oysters and add the liquor to the shrimp stock. Add enough water to make 7 or 8 cups of liquid at this point (depending on how thick you like your gumbo). Check the oysters for shell fragments.

Heat 1 tablespoon of the oil in a wide skillet (not nonstick) and add the okra. Sauté over medium heat, stirring occasionally, until all stickiness disappears, about 15 minutes. Remove from heat.

Heat the remaining oil in a large, heavy pot over high heat; add the flour and stir constantly until the roux begins to brown. Reduce the heat to medium or medium-low and cook, stirring constantly, until the roux is the color of dark chocolate.

Add the onions, the white parts of the green onions, the bell pepper, and the celery and cook, stirring, until translucent. Add the garlic and cook a minute more. Add the tomatoes and the oyster liquor, shrimp stock, and water combination until a slightly thickened and smooth consistency is achieved.

Add the okra, crabs, bay leaves, and Italian seasoning and season with salt, pepper, and Creole seasoning; cover and simmer for 40 minutes.

Add the shrimp and simmer for 5 more minutes. Add the oysters and simmer until they curl, about 3 minutes.

Turn off the heat, remove the bay leaves, and stir in most of the green onion tops and parsley, leaving some for garnish. Serve in bowls over the rice. Add pieces of the crab to each bowl and garnish with onion tops and parsley. Offer crab or nut crackers for the legs.

Chicken and Andouille Gumbo

If you've never cooked gumbo, chicken is the place to start. It's especially easy to make with boneless thighs. Or you can use whole pieces of bone-in chicken. Either way, a good sausage such as andouille, a Cajun specialty known for its smoky flavor and leanness, turns your gumbo into a bombshell of flavor.

MAKES 6–8 SERVINGS

2 pounds boneless chicken thighs, cut into bite-size chunks, or 1 whole chicken, cut into pieces

1 pound andouille sausage, cut into bite-size pieces

2 tablespoons plus 1/2 cup vegetable oil, divided

3/4 cup all-purpose flour

1 large onion, chopped

1 bunch green onions, chopped, white and green parts separated

1 green bell pepper, chopped

2 celery stalks, chopped

4 garlic cloves, minced

6 cups chicken stock

2 bay leaves

1 teaspoon Creole seasoning

Salt and freshly ground black pepper, to taste

1/3 cup chopped flat-leaf parsley

Cooked long-grain white rice, for serving

In a large, heavy pot, brown the chicken and andouille in 2 tablespoons of the oil. Remove the meat from the pot and set aside.

Add the remaining oil and the flour to the pot and stir constantly over high heat until the roux begins to brown. Reduce the heat to medium or medium-low and cook, stirring constantly, until the roux is the color of dark chocolate.

Add the onions, the white parts of the green onions, the bell pepper, the celery, and the garlic and sauté over low heat for about 5 minutes. Gradually stir in the chicken stock. Add the bay leaves and Creole seasoning and season with salt and pepper; cover and cook for about 45 minutes to 1 hour.

Add the green onion tops and parsley and remove the bay leaves. Serve in bowls over the rice with hot sauce and hot French bread.

Shrimp and Okra Gumbo

Creoles and Cajuns have long survived on this basic gumbo, and there is none better. The ingredients are pure Louisiana. Use fresh okra and shrimp if available, but frozen will run a close second. The only accompaniments needed are rice and French bread.

MAKES 8 SERVINGS

---

3 pounds small-to-medium shrimp in shells with heads or
   1½ pounds peeled and deveined frozen shrimp, thawed
1 pound fresh okra, cut into ¼-inch pieces, or frozen cut okra, thawed
1 tablespoon plus ½ cup vegetable oil, divided
½ cup all-purpose flour
1 large onion, chopped
1 bunch green onions, chopped, white and green parts separated
1 green bell pepper, chopped
2 celery stalks, chopped
3 large garlic cloves, minced
1 (14.5-ounce) can diced tomatoes
2 quarts shrimp stock or water
1½ teaspoons Creole seasoning
2 bay leaves
½ teaspoon dried thyme
¼ cup chopped flat-leaf parsley
Cooked long-grain white rice, for serving
French bread

If using fresh shrimp, de-head, peel, and devein them, placing the shells and heads in a medium pot. Add enough water to cover the shells by at least 2 inches and bring to a boil. Cover, reduce the heat to low, and simmer for 30 minutes. When slightly cooled, strain the stock into a large measuring cup and discard the shells.

If using fresh okra, heat 1 tablespoon of the oil in a medium-to-large skillet. Over medium heat, cook the okra, stirring occasionally, until the stringy liquid disappears. Set aside.

Heat the remaining oil in a large, heavy pot over high heat. Add the flour and stir constantly until the roux begins to brown. Reduce the heat to medium and cook, stirring constantly, until the roux is the color of milk chocolate. Add the onions and the white parts of the green onions and cook, stirring, until the onions begin to caramelize. Add the bell pepper and celery and cook until wilted. Add the garlic and cook a minute more.

Add the tomatoes and gradually stir in the stock or water. Add all the seasonings except the parsley, reduce the heat to low, cover, and simmer for 30 minutes. Add the shrimp and simmer until the shrimp turn pink, about 10 minutes. Remove from heat and add green onion tops and parsley and remove the bay leaves.

Serve in bowls over hot rice with hot French bread.

Super Gumbo

I was once a purist when it came to gumbo. My basic two were seafood, or chicken and sausage. I knew that some cooks put everything into the pot, but it wasn't until I created this recipe that I was won over. I even used both shrimp and chicken stock. It makes a huge pot and is great for taking half to a friend and saving half for your family.

MAKES 10–12 SERVINGS

2 pounds shrimp in shells with heads

1 pound fresh or frozen gumbo crabs, thawed if frozen

6 pieces chicken (such as legs and thighs)

Salt, pepper, and Creole seasoning, to taste

1 pound fresh okra, cut into pieces, or frozen cut okra, thawed

1 tablespoon plus 1 cup vegetable oil, divided

1 cup all-purpose flour

1 large onion, chopped

1 bunch green onions, chopped, white and green parts separated

1 green bell pepper, chopped

2 celery stalks, chopped

4 garlic cloves, minced

$\frac{1}{2}$ pound andouille or other smoked sausage, cut in quarters lengthwise and sliced $\frac{1}{4}$ inch thick

2 fresh tomatoes, diced, or 1 (14.5-ounce) can diced tomatoes

2 tablespoons tomato paste

9 cups seafood or chicken stock, or a combination of the two

3 bay leaves

$\frac{1}{2}$ teaspoon Creole seasoning

1 teaspoon salt

Several turns on a black pepper mill

2 tablespoons chopped flat-leaf parsley

Cooked long-grain white rice, for serving

De-head, peel, and devein the shrimp, placing the heads and shells in a medium pot. Add enough water to cover the shells by at least 2 inches and bring to a boil. Cover, reduce the heat, and simmer for 30 minutes. When slightly cooled, strain the stock into a large measuring cup and discard the shells.

Remove anything other than the shells containing the crab-meat from the crabs, leaving the legs on and the yellow and orange fat in place. If any parts of the shell need cleaning, do so with a sponge.

Rinse and dry the chicken pieces and sprinkle liberally with salt, pepper, and Creole seasoning.

In a medium skillet, heat 1 tablespoon of the vegetable oil; add the okra and cook over high heat, stirring frequently, until it begins to brown slightly. Reduce the heat to medium and continue cooking until the sticky liquid disappears.

In a large, heavy pot heat 2 tablespoons of the remaining oil and brown the chicken pieces on all sides. Remove the chicken and set aside.

Add the remaining oil and the flour to the pot and stir over high heat until the roux turns light brown. Reduce the heat to medium and cook, stirring constantly, until the roux is dark brown (the color of peanut butter or slightly darker). Be careful not to burn it.

Add the onions, the white parts of the green onions, the bell pepper, and the celery and cook, stirring, until translucent. Add the garlic and cook a minute more. Add the sausage, tomatoes, and tomato paste and cook another 5 minutes. Gradually stir in the stock.

Add all the seasonings except the parsley. Bring to a boil, then reduce the heat to a simmer. Cover and cook for about 1 hour and 20 minutes, stirring occasionally and skimming the fat off the top. Add the shrimp, parsley, and green onion tops, turn up the heat and cook for several minutes until the shrimp turn pink. Taste to adjust the seasonings and remove the bay leaves.

Serve in bowls over the cooked rice.

Cajun Hen Gumbo

Using a plump hen is a favorite way to make gumbo in the Cajun Country of southwest Louisiana. A fatty hen gives more flavor, and it is easy enough to skim the fat from the surface as the gumbo cooks. Cajuns generally serve the dish with whole pieces of the hen, but the meat can be taken off the bones after cooking, if preferred. Hens are tougher than chickens and must cook longer.

MAKES 6–8 SERVINGS

1 (5- to 6-pound) hen
Salt, freshly ground black pepper, and cayenne pepper,
   to taste
¾ cup vegetable oil, divided
½ pound andouille sausage, cut into ½-inch pieces
½ pound tasso, cut into ½-inch pieces
¾ cup all-purpose flour
2 medium onions, chopped
6 green onions, chopped, white and green parts separated
1 green bell pepper, chopped
3 celery stalks, chopped
1 tablespoon minced garlic
6½ cups chicken stock or water, or a combination of the two
3 bay leaves
Creole seasoning, to taste
3 tablespoons chopped flat-leaf parsley
Cooked long-grain white rice, for serving

Cut the hen into pieces as you would cut a chicken. Because the breast is large, cut it into 3 pieces. Use the back bone and any giblets, except the liver. Rinse, dry, and sprinkle liberally on all sides with salt and peppers.

Using a very large, heavy pot, heat ¼ cup of the oil and brown the hen well on all sides. Remove the hen from the pot and set aside.

Add the remaining oil and the flour to the pot and stir constantly over high heat until the roux turns light brown. Reduce the heat to medium and cook, stirring constantly, until the roux is dark brown (the color of milk chocolate or a little darker).

Reduce the heat to low; add the onions, the white parts of the green onions, the bell pepper, the celery, and the garlic and sauté until translucent. Gradually stir in the stock and/or water. Add the bay leaves and season with Creole seasoning, cover, and simmer for 3 hours, stirring occasionally. As the gumbo cooks, skim the fat from the surface. You may skim as much as 1 cup of fat.

When the gumbo is cooked and the hen is tender, remove the bay leaves and stir in the green onion tops and parsley. Serve in bowls over the rice.

Quail Gumbo

I have known two chefs who made this gumbo, the late Chris Kera-georgiou of La Provence restaurant on the north shore of Lake Ponchartrain, and John Folse of Donaldsonville, Louisiana. Kera-georgiou claimed to have invented it, and Folse calls his Death by Gumbo. It is time-consuming to make but worth it, especially if you know a quail hunter. If not, you can buy them frozen in some grocery stores and at farmers' markets.

MAKES 8 SERVINGS

8 fresh quail or frozen, thawed
Salt and freshly ground black pepper, to taste
1 pound boudin or about 4 cups homemade jambalaya
    (or use a quick mix like Zatarain's or Oak Grove)
¾ cup vegetable oil
¾ cup all-purpose flour
1 large onion, chopped
3 green onions, chopped, white and green parts separated
1 green bell pepper, chopped
4 large garlic cloves, minced
¼ pound tasso or andouille (or other smoked) sausage,
    cut into bite-size pieces
2 tablespoons tomato paste
6 cups homemade or canned chicken stock
1 teaspoon dried thyme
3 bay leaves
½ teaspoon Creole seasoning
½ teaspoon celery salt
3 tablespoons chopped flat-leaf parsley

Rinse the quail and remove any remaining feathers. Dry well and season with salt and pepper inside and out. If using boudin, remove it from the casings. Stuff each quail with about 4 tablespoons boudin or jambalaya and tie string around each quail from back to front, crossing the legs to hold in the stuffing.

In a wide, heavy pot, heat 3 tablespoons of the oil and carefully brown the quail lightly on all sides, moving them about to keep the skin from sticking. Remove the quail from the pot and set aside.

Add the remaining oil and the flour to the pot and stir constantly over medium-high heat until the roux begins to brown. Reduce the heat to medium and cook, stirring constantly, until the roux is the color of peanut butter.

Reduce the heat to low and add the onions and the white parts of the green onions, caramelizing them for about 5 minutes. Add the bell pepper and cook until wilted. Add the garlic and cook 1 more minute. Add the tomato paste and tasso and cook a few minutes more. Gradually stir in the stock, followed by all the seasonings except the green onion tops and parsley. Bring to a boil and then reduce the heat to medium-low.

Return the quail to the pot, cover, and simmer for 30 minutes. When done, add the green onion tops and remove the bay leaves.

To serve, place 1 quail in each bowl of gumbo and sprinkle with parsley.

Gumbo z'Herbes

Greens gumbo once was a Lenten dish made without meat. Because seasoning meat so naturally complements greens, most cooks can't resist adding smoked ham. The number of different kinds of greens you use in this dish is said to predict the number of new friends you will make in the coming year. The magic numbers are seven and nine. An even number is said to bring bad luck. Gumbo z'Herbes bears similarities to French, German and West African dishes. In New Orleans, it was traditionally served on Good Friday and now often on Holy Thursday, the Thursday before Easter. It is at its most delicious when dark greens are in season.

MAKES 8 SERVINGS

1 small ham bone or ½ pound smoked ham cubes

1 pint shucked oysters with their liquor

½ cup vegetable oil

½ cup all-purpose flour

1 large onion, chopped

3 green onions, chopped

3 celery stalks, chopped

3 garlic cloves, minced

½ teaspoon Creole seasoning

3 bay leaves

½ teaspoon dried thyme

1 tablespoon sugar

2 cups cleaned and roughly chopped mustard greens

2 cups cleaned and roughly chopped turnip greens

4 cups cleaned and roughly chopped collard greens

4 cups spinach

1 bunch flat-leaf parsley

½ small cabbage, chopped or shredded

2 cups endive, torn in pieces

Salt and freshly ground black pepper, to taste

Cooked long-grain white rice, for serving

If using a ham bone, simmer it in a large pot in 2 quarts of water, covered, for 2 hours or until the meat is about to fall off the bone. When cool enough to handle, remove the meat from the bone and set aside. Discard the bone and save the stock (you will need about 7 cups).

Strain the oysters, reserving their liquor, and check for shell fragments. You should have about ½ cup of liquor.

In a very large, heavy pot, combine the oil and flour and stir over high heat until the roux starts to brown. Reduce the heat to medium and cook, stirring constantly, until the roux becomes the color of milk chocolate. Immediately add the onions and simmer until caramelized. Add the celery and garlic and simmer a minute more.

Stir in the reserved ham stock, oyster liquor (about ½ cup), Creole seasoning, bay leaves, thyme, sugar, reserved ham or ham cubes, and greens and season with salt and pepper. Simmer, covered, for about 1 hour. Add the oysters and cook until they curl, about 1 minute. Taste and adjust the seasonings. Turn off the heat and remove the bay leaves.

Serve in soup bowls over the rice.

Filé Gumbo

There are mixed rules about thickening gumbo with a roux, filé powder, or okra. The fact is that different cooks might use one, two, or all three of the thickeners. Generally, most cooks use either filé or okra, plus a roux. A hard and fast rule, also occasionally violated, is never add the filé until after the gumbo is cooked. It can be mixed into the pot of gumbo or individually added to the serving bowls. If you intend to eat all of the gumbo at once, add it to the pot; if you expect leftovers, put it in the bowls. If reheated, filé tends to get ropey. For this gumbo, I am using crabmeat rather than whole crabs. It is more expensive this way but some people prefer it to having crabs in their bowls.

MAKES 6–8 SERVINGS

---

2 pounds shrimp in shells with heads

$\frac{1}{2}$ cup vegetable oil or bacon drippings

$\frac{1}{2}$ cup all-purpose flour

1 onion, chopped

1 green bell pepper, chopped

3 garlic cloves, minced

2 tablespoons tomato paste

2 bay leaves

$\frac{1}{2}$ teaspoon salt, or to taste

$\frac{1}{2}$ teaspoon freshly ground black pepper, or to taste

$\frac{1}{2}$ teaspoon cayenne pepper, or to taste

2 tablespoons filé powder

1 pound jumbo lump crabmeat

Cooked long-grain white rice, for serving

De-head, peel, and devein the shrimp, placing the heads and shells in a medium pot. Add enough water to cover the shells by at least 2 inches and bring to a boil. Cover, reduce the heat, and simmer for 30 minutes. When slightly cooled, strain the stock into a large measuring cup and discard the shells. If necessary, add enough water to the stock to make 5 cups of liquid. Set aside.

In a large, heavy pot, combine the oil and flour. Stir constantly over high heat until the flour begins to brown. Reduce the heat to medium and stir constantly until the roux turns dark brown.

Add the onions and bell pepper and cook until wilted. Add the garlic and cook a minute more. Stir in the tomato paste and simmer for 5 minutes, stirring occasionally. Gradually stir in the shrimp stock. Add all the seasonings except the filé, cover, and simmer over low heat for 30 minutes.

Add the shrimp and continue cooking for 3 minutes if the shrimp are small or 7 minutes if large. Turn off the heat. If you are serving all of the gumbo immediately, add the filé and mix well. (If not, reserve the filé to add to individual bowls.) Gently stir in the crabmeat.

Serve in bowls over the hot rice. If you have not added the filé, add ½–¾ teaspoon to each bowl, depending on the size of the bowls.

Catfish Gumbo

This easy-to-make gumbo requires none of the efforts of finding fresh shrimp and crabs or of peeling shellfish. Because of catfish farming in the South, the fish is readily available in grocery stores everywhere.

MAKES 6–8 SERVINGS

3 pounds catfish nuggets, divided

$\frac{1}{2}$ cup canola or other vegetable oil

$\frac{1}{2}$ cup all-purpose flour

1 large onion, chopped, peels and trimmings reserved

1 green bell pepper, chopped, seeds and trimmings reserved

2 celery stalks, chopped

6 green onions, chopped, white and green parts separated

3 large garlic cloves, minced

1 (10-ounce) can original Ro-tel tomatoes with chilies

2 cups chopped fresh or canned diced tomatoes

3 cups stock

$\frac{1}{2}$ cup white wine

3 bay leaves

$\frac{1}{2}$ teaspoon dried thyme

1 teaspoon fresh lemon juice

$\frac{1}{2}$ teaspoon Worcestershire sauce

$1\frac{1}{2}$ teaspoons Creole seasoning

Salt and freshly ground pepper, to taste

2 tablespoons chopped flat-leaf parsley

Cooked long-grain white rice, for serving

Cut 2 pounds of the catfish nuggets into 1-inch cubes and set aside. Place the remaining nuggets in a small pot with 4 cups of water and the trimmings from the vegetables to make stock. Cover and simmer for 45 minutes. Strain the stock into a large measuring cup and discard the solids.

Heat the oil in a large, heavy pot. Add the flour and stir constantly over medium heat to make a medium-dark roux the color of peanut butter. Add the onion, the white parts of the green onions, the bell pepper, and the celery and cook until wilted. Add the garlic and cook 1 minute more.

Add the tomatoes, 3 cups of the stock, the wine, bay leaves, thyme, lemon juice, Worcestershire sauce, and Creole seasoning and season with salt and pepper. Bring to a boil. Reduce the heat, cover, and simmer for 30 minutes, stirring occasionally.

Add the cubed catfish and bring to a boil. Reduce the heat and simmer until the fish is cooked through, about 5 minutes. Remove the bay leaves and add the parsley and green onion tops. Cover and let the gumbo rest for an hour or so.

Reheat the gumbo and serve in bowls over the rice.

Cabbage Gumbo

This age-old gumbo has been served to rich and poor, fancied up with round steak or flavored with a piece of salt pork. Smoked ham or sausages are most commonly used.

MAKES 4–6 SERVINGS

1 large cabbage (about 3 pounds)

4 thick slices bacon

¼ cup vegetable oil (more or less as needed)

½ cup all-purpose flour

1 onion, chopped

1 green bell pepper, chopped

2 celery stalks, chopped

3 large garlic cloves, minced

Salt and freshly ground black pepper, to taste

1 teaspoon sugar

3 bay leaves

1 teaspoon Creole seasoning

8 cups water

1 (10-ounce) can original Ro-tel tomatoes with green chilies

2 small smoked ham hocks

Cooked long-grain white rice, for serving

Cut the cabbage into bite-size pieces; rinse, drain, and set aside.

In a large, heavy pot, cook the bacon until crisp. Remove the bacon from the pot and reserve. Carefully pour the bacon grease into a large measuring cup and add enough oil to make ½ cup. Return the grease to the pan and add the flour; stir constantly over medium heat to make a light-brown or butterscotch-colored roux.

Add the onions, bell pepper, and celery and sauté until wilted. Add the garlic and sauté a minute more. Stir in the remaining ingredients and the cabbage and bring to a boil. Reduce the heat, cover, and simmer for 1 hour, stirring occasionally.

Serve in bowls over the rice and top with crumbled reserved bacon. Serve hot sauce on the side.

Turkey Gumbo

A lot of people in south Louisiana say that their favorite part of the Thanksgiving feast is the turkey gumbo the next day. I have known people who put all of the leftover dressing and gravy in the gumbo. It is a blessed relief after the overdose of calories the day before to settle down to a simple bowl of gumbo. However, the locals don't eat anything bland. This gumbo is almost always spiced up with andouille sausage. Adding oysters to the gumbo makes it a superb dish.

MAKES 6–8 SERVINGS

1 or more turkey carcasses and leftover turkey

$\frac{1}{2}$ cup vegetable oil

$\frac{1}{2}$ cup all-purpose flour

1 onion, chopped

1 bunch green onions, chopped

3 celery stalks, chopped

3 garlic cloves, minced

Leftover turkey gravy (optional)

2 bay leaves

$\frac{1}{2}$ teaspoon dried thyme

Salt, Creole seasoning, and freshly ground black pepper, to taste

$\frac{1}{2}$ pound andouille (or other smoked) sausage, cut into bite-size pieces

1 pint shucked oysters (optional)

3 tablespoons chopped flat-leaf parsley

Cooked long-grain white rice, for serving

Remove any meat from the turkey carcass. Cut into chunks, along with leftover turkey. Set aside.

Place the turkey bones in a stock pot, cover with water, and bring to a boil. Reduce the heat to low, cover, and simmer for 1 hour. When cool enough to handle, strain the stock into a large measuring cup and discard the bones. If using oysters, strain the oyster liquor into the stock. If necessary, add water to make at least 8 cups of liquid. Set aside.

In a large, heavy pot, heat the oil over medium-high heat. Add the flour and stir constantly until the roux begins to brown. Reduce the heat to medium and cook, stirring constantly, until the roux becomes the color of peanut butter.

Add the onions and celery and simmer over low heat until translucent. Add the garlic and cook a minute more. Add 8 cups of the stock (or more if you prefer a thinner gumbo; if you have leftover turkey gravy, add it at this point).

Add all of the seasonings (except the parsley) and the sausage; cover and simmer for 30 minutes. Add the turkey meat and oysters, if using, and cook until the oysters curl, 1–2 minutes. Remove the bay leaves and adjust the seasonings. Add the parsley and serve in bowls over the rice.

Roux-less Gumbo

This gumbo maintains the thickness of a gumbo without the oil and flour that make a thickening roux. That's good news for dieters, and it saves time for the busy cook. Browning the chicken adds flavor, while filé, which is made of sassafras leaves, and plenty of okra give the gumbo body.

MAKES 6–8 SERVINGS

2 pounds medium shrimp in shells with heads or 1 pound
    peeled and deveined frozen shrimp, thawed
3 cups sliced fresh okra or 3 cups frozen cut okra, thawed
1 pound boneless chicken thighs, cut into 1-inch pieces
Creole seasoning for sprinkling chicken plus $\frac{1}{2}$ teaspoon
1 teaspoon plus 3 tablespoons vegetable oil
1 large onion, chopped
1 green bell pepper, chopped
1 bunch green onions, chopped, green and white parts
    separated
2 celery stalks, chopped
3 garlic cloves, minced
1 (15-ounce) can crushed tomatoes
4 cups shrimp and/or chicken stock
$\frac{1}{2}$ teaspoon salt
10 grinds on a black pepper mill
1 teaspoon celery salt
1 heaping tablespoon chopped flat-leaf parsley
1 tablespoon filé powder
Cooked long-grain white rice, for serving

If using fresh shrimp, remove the heads and shells and devein the shrimp. Place the shells and heads in a medium pot, add enough water to cover the shells by at least 2 inches, and bring to a boil. Cover, reduce the heat to low, and simmer for 30 minutes. When slightly cooled, strain the stock into a large measuring cup and discard the shells. You'll need 4 cups of stock. Reserve the rest for a later use.

Heat 1 teaspoon of the oil in a skillet over medium heat and add the okra. Cook, turning often, until all the sliminess is removed from okra. Set aside.

Sprinkle the chicken on all sides with Creole seasoning. Heat the remaining oil in large, heavy pot and, in 2 batches, brown the chicken pieces on all sides. Remove the chicken to a plate.

Add the onion, the white parts of the green onions, the bell pepper, and the celery to the pot and sauté until translucent. Add the garlic and sauté a minute more.

Return the chicken to the pot and add the okra, tomatoes, stock, remaining Creole seasoning, salt, pepper, and celery salt. Cover and simmer for 30 minutes.

Add the shrimp, green onion tops, and parsley and cook 5–10 minutes longer, or until the shrimp are just pink. Add the filé to the pot if you intend to serve all the gumbo. Serve in bowls over the rice. If you have not added the filé, add ½–¾ teaspoon to each bowl.

Duck and Andouille Gumbo

South Louisiana is at the base of the Mississippi Flyway, where multitudes of waterfowl end their migration journeys, to the delight of local hunters. Ducks and geese are the fodder of many delicious dishes, particularly gumbos that are often cooked right at the hunting camps. If you don't have a hunter in the family, domestic duck will work just as well. Wild ducks are tougher and require longer cooking. It's best to make the stock and debone the duck a day in advance.

MAKES 6–8 SERVINGS

1 (6-pound) duckling
2 onions, 1 quartered and the other chopped
4 celery stalks, 2 cut in chunks and the other 2 chopped
4 bay leaves, divided
Freshly ground black pepper, to taste
1 pound andouille sausage, cut into bite-size pieces
3/4 cup vegetable oil
1 cup all-purpose flour
1 bunch green onions, chopped, white and green parts
    separated
1 green bell pepper, chopped
4 garlic cloves, minced
1/2 teaspoon dried thyme
1/2 teaspoon Creole seasoning
1/4 teaspoon cayenne pepper
1 tablespoon Worcestershire sauce
Salt, to taste
1/2 cup chopped flat-leaf parsley
Cooked long-grain white rice, for serving

Rinse the duck and remove any excess fat. Place the duck in a large pot and cover with water. Add the quartered onion, celery chunks, 2 of the bay leaves, and several grinds on a pepper mill. Bring to a boil. Reduce the heat to low and simmer until the duck has cooked through, about 45 minutes. Remove the duck from that pot and let rest until cool enough to handle. Debone the duck and cut the meat into bite-size pieces. Set the meat aside.

Return the bones to the pot and simmer for 1 hour. Strain the stock into a large bowl and let cool. Refrigerate until the fat hardens and skim and discard the fat.

In a large skillet, brown the sausage over medium-high heat. Set aside.

Heat the oil in a large, heavy pot over high heat; add the flour and stir constantly until the roux begins to brown. Reduce the heat to medium or medium-low and cook, stirring constantly, until the roux is the color of dark chocolate.

Add the chopped onion, the white parts of the green onions, the celery, and the bell pepper and cook, stirring, until wilted. Add the garlic and cook a minute more. Gradually stir in 6 cups of the stock. (If you have extra stock, freeze it for another use.) Add the remaining bay leaves and the thyme, Creole seasoning, cayenne pepper, and Worcestershire sauce and season with salt.

Add the sausage and duck and simmer, covered, until the duck is tender, about 1 hour. Stir in the parsley and green onion tops.

Serve in bowls over the rice with hot sauce and hot French bread on the side.

Chef Tory McPhail's Braised Goose and Foie Gras Jambalaya

Chef Tory McPhail received the James Beard Foundation's Best Chef South award in 2013. He is executive chef of the world-famous Commander's Palace restaurant in New Orleans's Garden District. This unique version of jambalaya, developed by McPhail, is a special-occasion recipe if you have to buy domestic goose, which is very expensive. In Louisiana, geese are popular game for hunters, who often use them in jambalaya and gumbo.

MAKES 4–6 SERVINGS

1 cup goose meat

6 ounces foie gras, chopped

12 garlic cloves, peeled and minced

1 onion, medium diced

2 green bell peppers, medium diced

6 celery stalks, medium diced

2 bay leaves

1 teaspoon cayenne pepper

4 tablespoons kosher salt, or to taste

½ cup red wine

2 cups rice

4 cups poultry stock

1 tablespoon chopped fresh sage

1 tablespoon chopped fresh thyme

Cook the goose meat in a medium skillet over high heat, stirring, until it has browned. Reduce the heat to low, add a small amount of water, cover tightly, and cook until the meat is tender, about 1–2 hours.

Place a heavy-bottom braising pan over medium-high heat. Add the foie gras to the pan and swirl to melt for 5 seconds. Add the garlic, onion, bell pepper, celery, bay leaves, cayenne, and salt. Swirl evenly with a wooden spoon for 3–5 minutes or until the onion is translucent and the vegetables are soft and starting to brown.

Add the wine and stir constantly to deglaze the pan, allowing the liquid to completely evaporate.

Add the meat, rice, and stock, and bring the jambalaya to a simmer. Reduce the heat, cover the pan, and cook for 10 minutes. Turn off the heat, keep the pan covered, and continue to steam until the rice is cooked all the way. Fluff the rice with a fork, and add the sage and thyme.

Bad Bart's Black Jambalaya

Bart Bell says he never uses a recipe for jambalaya because he uses what he has on hand. "It's a leftover dish. That's why there are so many varieties," he says. At the Crescent City Pie and Sausage Co. (which is now closed) in New Orleans, chef-owner Bell made his from his homemade sausages and slow-smoked meats that were also served in the restaurant. Bell grew up in south Louisiana along Bayou Teche, where he grew up eating Cajun-style home cooking. His popular restaurant also is known for its turnover-style pies filled with such stuffings as crawfish, duck confit, curried eggplant, or braised greens. There are several reasons why his jambalaya is called "black." He makes it in a black iron (or cast-iron) pot and uses smoked pork butt that has caramelized and charred black on the edges. Unlike the Creole red version, his jambalaya contains no tomatoes, and it contains black-eyed peas. The following is as close as he comes to a recipe. He says that Uncle Ben's rice works best for him.

MAKES 10–12 SERVINGS

¼ cup vegetable oil

1 pound Louisiana smoked sausage, such as andouille, chaurice, or green onion, cut into ¼-inch-thick rounds

1 large onion, diced

3 celery stalks, diced

2 poblano peppers, diced

¼ cup minced garlic

½ pound smoked pork butt (see Note)

½ pound smoked chicken thighs (see Note)

1 (12-ounce) can black-eyed peas

4 cups stock, preferably pork (see Note)

2 tablespoons chopped fresh oregano

2 tablespoons chopped flat-leaf parsley

2 tablespoons chopped fresh thyme

1 tablespoon kosher salt

1 teaspoon freshly ground black pepper

1 teaspoon cayenne pepper

2 cups Uncle Ben's long-grain rice

In a large, heavy pot, preferably black cast) iron, heat the oil over medium heat. Add the sausage and cook until it curls. Add the onions, celery, peppers, and garlic and sauté until translucent. Add the pork and cook 5 minutes, stirring frequently. Add the chicken and cook another 5 minutes. Add the black-eyed peas and cook another 5 minutes.

Add stock and bring to a simmer. Add the herbs and seasonings and then the rice and bring to a simmer. Cover and cook over low heat until the rice is done, about 30 minutes.

NOTE ✳ If you don't want to smoke the pork or chicken, you can braise it. To braise the pork, rub it with salt and pepper and brown it on all sides in a black iron skillet, then cook it in water on the stovetop or in the oven until the meat falls off the bone. You can then use the braising liquid for the stock. To prepare the chicken, rub it with salt and pepper and brown it on all sides over high temperature until it caramelizes and is 75 percent cooked before adding it in bite-size chunks to the jambalaya.

Chicken, Shrimp, and Sausage Jambalaya

Jambalaya serves a crowd and people of all ages love it. The most popular version contains chicken, shrimp, and smoked sausage. Some cooks use whole pieces of chicken on the bone; others prefer to cook and debone the chicken (or purchase a rotisseried one and debone it). Louisiana folks like jambalaya spicy, served with hot French bread and cold beer. If you are serving this to an all-ages crowd, save the hot sauce for the table.

MAKES 6–8 SERVINGS

1 chicken, cut into 10 pieces, splitting the breast into fourths
Salt, freshly ground black pepper, and Creole seasoning,
    to taste
¼ cup vegetable oil
1 pound smoked sausage, preferably pork, cut into ¼-inch-
    thick rounds
1 large onion, chopped
6 green onions, chopped, green and white parts separated
1 green bell pepper, chopped
2 celery stalks, chopped
4 garlic cloves, minced
3 cups water, or more as needed
½ teaspoon salt
½ teaspoon freshly ground black pepper
1 tablespoon Creole seasoning
1½ cups long-grain white rice
2 pounds shrimp, peeled and deveined, or 1 pound medium
    peeled and deveined frozen shrimp, thawed
⅓ cup minced Italian flat-leaf parsley

Rinse the chicken pieces and pat dry. Season on all sides with salt, freshly ground black pepper, and Creole seasoning. Heat the oil in a large, heavy pot. When hot, brown the chicken on all sides and remove to paper towels. Brown the sausage and remove from pot.

If necessary, add enough extra oil to cover the bottom of pot. Add the onion, the white parts of the green onions, the bell pepper, and the celery and sauté until transparent. Add the garlic and sauté a minute more. Add the water and seasonings and bring to a boil over high heat. Add the rice, cover, and reduce the heat to low. Simmer for 20 minutes. Gently stir in the shrimp (at this point, there still should be some liquid at the bottom of the pot. If not, add ¼ cup water for moisture while the shrimp cook), the green onion tops, and the parsley and simmer 10 more minutes, or until the water has been absorbed. Stir gently so as not to break up the ingredients.

Serve hot with hot French bread and salad and Louisiana hot sauce on the side.

Crawfish and Sausage Jambalaya

I've almost exclusively used shrimp as the seafood component of jambalaya, but now I know that crawfish is just as good. Although Chinese imports are cheaper, in Louisiana, we like to use our own crawfish tails, which are packed with fat from the heads. Smoked sausage adds another dimension of flavor, but ham or chicken could be used just as well.

MAKES 8–10 SERVINGS

3 tablespoons vegetable oil

1 medium onion, chopped

1 bunch green onions, chopped, white and green parts separated

1 green bell pepper, chopped

2 celery stalks, chopped

3 garlic cloves, minced

1 pound smoked sausage, cut into $\frac{1}{4}$-inch-thick rounds

1 (14.5-ounce) can diced tomatoes

1 tablespoon tomato paste

3 cups seafood stock, preferably, or chicken stock or water

$\frac{1}{2}$ teaspoon dried thyme

$\frac{1}{4}$ teaspoon Creole seasoning

$\frac{1}{2}$ teaspoon salt

$\frac{1}{2}$ teaspoon freshly ground black pepper

1 teaspoon Worcestershire sauce

$1\frac{1}{2}$ cups rice

1 pound Louisiana crawfish tails with fat

2 tablespoons chopped flat-leaf parsley

Heat the oil in a large, heavy pot. Add the onion, the white parts of the green onions, the bell pepper, and the celery and sauté until transparent. Add the garlic and sausage and sauté a couple of minutes more. Add the tomatoes, tomato paste, and stock and bring to a boil. Add the seasonings except the parsley, reduce the heat to low, cover, and simmer for 5 minutes. Return to a boil and add the rice. Reduce the heat again and simmer, covered, for 10 minutes. Add the crawfish and green onion tops and simmer until the liquid has been absorbed, about 20 more minutes. Remove from the heat and top with the parsley.

Pastalaya

Pastalaya is a form of jambalaya that uses pasta instead of rice. The pasta can be cooked separately but is commonly cooked along with the other ingredients, making it a one-pot meal. Shrimp or pork is often added to or substituted for the chicken.

MAKES 6–8 SERVINGS

---

3 tablespoons vegetable oil such as canola

½ pound smoked sausage, cut into ½-inch-thick rounds

2 boneless, skinless chicken breasts, cut into bite-size cubes

1 large onion, chopped

½ green bell pepper, chopped

2 celery stalks, chopped

6 green onions, chopped

3 large garlic cloves, minced

1 (14.5-ounce) can diced tomatoes

3 cups chicken broth, homemade or canned

½ teaspoon dried thyme

½ teaspoon Creole seasoning

Salt and freshly ground black pepper, to taste

12 ounces spaghetti or other pasta

Heat the oil to hot in a large, heavy pot. Brown the sausage on both sides over high heat and remove from the pot. Brown the chicken cubes and remove from pot. Reduce the heat to medium heat sauté the onion, bell pepper, celery, and green onions until wilted. Add the garlic and sauté a minute more. Add the tomatoes and chicken broth and return the sausage and chicken to the pot. Simmer, covered, for 15 minutes.

Add the pasta and stir it into the liquid. Simmer, covered, over medium-low heat, stirring occasionally, for 15 more minutes, or until the pasta is al dente and has absorbed most of the liquid.

Slow Cooker Jambalaya

Slow cooking is not the usual way to cook jambalaya but is a good way for working families to have a hearty meal when they get home. Another option is to cook the rice separately, reducing the broth to one cup and serving the sauce over the rice. I sometimes add shrimp to this dish to make it extra tasty.

MAKES 6–8 SERVINGS

1½ pounds boneless chicken thighs, rinsed, trimmed of
    excess fat, and cut into 1-inch cubes
3 links Cajun smoked sausage (about 14 ounces total),
    cut into ¼-inch-thick rounds
1 medium onion, chopped
1 green bell pepper, chopped
1 celery stalk, chopped
3 garlic cloves, minced
2 tablespoons tomato paste
1 teaspoon Creole seasoning
1 teaspoon salt
½ teaspoon freshly ground black pepper
½ teaspoon Tabasco sauce
½ teaspoon Worcestershire sauce
2 cups chicken broth
1½ cups long-grain rice
2 pounds medium shrimp, peeled and deveined (optional)

Place all the ingredients (except the shrimp, if using) into a slow cooker. Stir together, cover, and cook on low for 5 hours.

If using shrimp, gently stir them in after the 5 hours of cooking and cook on high for 30 minutes to 1 hour more, or until the shrimp are done but not overcooked.

Lagniappe

Just as gumbo and jambalaya are unique to
south Louisiana, so are many other dishes, like corn
maque choux or crawfish pies, that draw hundreds
of thousands of people to the city annually.

Alligator Sauce Piquant

Southwest Louisiana settlers are known for making a sauce pi-quant, the Cajun French term for a spicy sauce. This tomato-based sauce can be made with poultry, fish, or game and is one of the tastiest ways to serve alligator, which is officially classified as a seafood. Lighter colored tail meat, sometimes called alligator ten-derloin or filet, is quick-cooking and delicious. Once the sauce is made, it is usually served over rice.

MAKES 6–8 SERVINGS

2 pounds boneless, trimmed alligator, cut into 1-inch pieces
Salt and freshly ground black pepper, to taste
2 tablespoons plus ½ cup vegetable oil, divided
¾ cup all-purpose flour
1 large onion, chopped
1 bunch green onions, chopped, white and green parts
    separated
1 green bell pepper, chopped
2 celery stalks, chopped
4 garlic cloves, minced
2 large fresh tomatoes, in season, peeled and chopped,
    or 1 (14-ounce) can chopped plum tomatoes
1 (10-ounce) can original Ro-tel tomatoes
Juice of 1 lemon
2 tablespoons Worcestershire sauce
1 teaspoon salt
½ teaspoon freshly ground black pepper
¼ teaspoon cayenne pepper
2 bay leaves
2 cups beef stock
⅓ cup chopped flat-leaf parsley
Cooked long-grain white rice, for serving

Season the alligator with salt and pepper. Heat 2 tablespoons of the oil in a large skillet, add the alligator pieces, and sear on all sides. The meat will not turn brown. Remove the alligator and set aside. Save the pan for later deglazing.

Heat the remaining oil in a large, heavy pot over medium-high heat; add the flour and stir constantly until the roux begins to brown. Reduce the heat to medium and cook, stirring constantly, until the roux turns a reddish-brown color. Immediately add the onion, the white parts of the green onions, the bell peppers, and the celery and sauté over medium-low heat until translucent. Add the garlic and sauté a minute more. Return the alligator to the pot.

Meanwhile, heat a little of the stock in the skillet over high heat to deglaze. Stir the liquid, being sure to scrape up the brown bits from the bottom of the skillet, and add this to the pot.

Add the rest of the ingredients except the parsley to the pot. Cover and simmer over low heat, stirring occasionally, until the meat is tender, about 30 minutes. Adjust the seasonings, add the green onion tops and parsley, and remove the bay leaves. Serve over the hot rice.

Calas

In the early twentieth century, elderly women wearing bandanas sold tasty rice fritters on the streets of the New Orleans French Quarter, often carrying their wares in baskets on top of their heads and shouting "Belle Cala! Tout Chaud." The rice cakes were commonly eaten with cups of café au lait. The custom continues, but the rice cakes have been replaced by beignets and they're eaten in cafés. Both are delicious pastries dusted in powdered sugar. The difference is that beignets contain no rice.

MAKES 30 CALAS

½ cup all-purpose flour
2½ teaspoons baking powder
⅓ cup sugar
½ teaspoon salt
½ teaspoon freshly grated nutmeg
3 eggs
1 teaspoon vanilla
2 cups cooked long-grain white rice
Vegetable oil for deep frying
Confectioners' sugar to sprinkle

In a large bowl, whisk together the flour, baking powder, sugar, salt, and nutmeg. Add the eggs and vanilla and mix well. Stir in the rice.

In a large frying pan or deep fryer, heat the oil to 360°. Carefully drop the mixture by teaspoonfuls into the hot oil in batches. Fry the dough, turning often, until golden brown, and remove to paper towels. Sprinkle with confectioners' sugar and serve hot.

Corn Maque Choux

A colorful summer side dish, this fresh-corn approach to creamed corn is so good you won't be able to stop eating it. The key is cutting through half the kernels of corn and scraping the rest. Some cooks add cream, but I think the creaminess of the scraped corn is enough.

MAKES 8 SERVINGS

6–8 ears yellow corn
2 tablespoons butter
1 green bell pepper, chopped
1 medium onion, chopped
1 large tomato, chopped
2 garlic cloves, minced
¾ cup water
Pinch cayenne pepper
1 teaspoon sugar
Salt and freshly ground black pepper, to taste

Rinse and clear the corn of silks. Using a very sharp knife over a wide bowl, cut through the kernels halfway to the cob. Use a table knife to scrape the juices from the remaining part of kernels. Set aside.

In a large, heavy skillet or medium pot, heat the butter and sauté the bell pepper and onion until translucent. Add the tomato and garlic and cook over medium heat for 5 minutes. Add the water, corn, cayenne pepper, and sugar and season with salt and pepper. Bring to a boil, reduce heat to low, cover, and simmer until corn is done, about 30 minutes. Taste and adjust seasonings.

Corn and Shrimp Soup

Try this soup during corn season, and you'll love the fresh, sweet taste, which is so much better than the flavor of the canned corn called for in many recipes. Corn matches well with both shrimp and crab, especially in soups popular in New Orleans restaurants.

MAKES 8 SERVINGS

2 pounds medium shrimp in shells with heads

8 ears corn

1 stick butter

½ cup all-purpose flour

1 large onion, chopped

3 green onions, chopped, white and green parts separated

1 green bell pepper, chopped

2 celery stalks, chopped

1 teaspoon minced garlic

1 (10-ounce) can original Ro-Tel tomatoes and green chilies

Salt, freshly ground black pepper, and Creole seasoning,
    to taste

½ pint heavy cream

2 tablespoons chopped flat-leaf parsley

De-head, peel, and devein the shrimp, placing the heads and shells into a large pot. Set the shrimp aside in the refrigerator.

Using a very sharp knife, cut the kernels off the corn cobs into a very large bowl. Using a dull table knife, scrape the cobs to release all of the corn juice into the bowl. Set aside.

Add the corn cobs to the pot with the shrimp peelings. Add enough water to cover the shells and cobs and bring to a boil. Reduce the heat to medium and simmer for 30 minutes, uncovered. When slightly cooled, strain the stock into a large measuring cup and discard the shells and cobs. You should have 8 cups of stock; if not, add enough water to make 8 cups of liquid.

In a large, heavy pot, melt the butter over medium heat; add the flour and cook, stirring constantly, until the roux turns the color of butterscotch.

Add the onion, the white parts of the green onions, the bell pepper, the celery, and the garlic and cook until the onions are translucent. Add the tomatoes and gradually stir in the stock. Season with salt, pepper, and Creole seasoning and simmer, covered, for about 15 minutes. Add the corn and cook 10 minutes longer. Add the shrimp and cook until they are pink, about 2 minutes. Add the cream, green onion tops, and parsley. When ready to serve, heat gently. Do not boil.

Crab and Brie Soup

This rich and delicious soup was created by Kim Kringlie, chef-owner of Dakota Restaurant in Covington. For years, it was a favorite at the New Orleans Wine & Food Experience. My version substitutes half-and-half for heavy cream as the brie makes it rich enough for me.

MAKES 6 SERVINGS

1 (1-pound) package frozen gumbo crabs
1 stick butter
1/2 cup all-purpose flour
1 medium onion, chopped
2 celery stalks, chopped
3 garlic cloves, minced
4 cups crab stock
1/2 cup dry white wine
1 bay leaf
1 teaspoon Worcestershire sauce
10 turns on a black pepper mill
1 teaspoon Creole seasoning
Salt, to taste
1/2 pound Brie cheese, rind removed
1 1/2 cups half-and-half
1 pound lump crabmeat

Place the gumbo crabs (no need to thaw them) in a medium pot, cover with water, and bring to a boil. Cover, reduce the heat, and simmer for 45 minutes. Strain the stock into a large measuring cup. If necessary, add enough water to make 4 cups.

Melt the butter in a large, heavy pot over medium heat; add the flour and stir constantly until the roux turns light brown. Add the onion and celery and cook, stirring occasionally, for 5 minutes. Add the garlic and cook a minute more. Gradually stir in the stock and wine; add the bay leaf, Worcestershire sauce, pepper, and Creole seasoning and season with salt. Cover and simmer for 15 minutes.

Tear or cut the Brie into small pieces and whisk into the soup over low heat until melted. Stir in the half-and-half. Pick over the lump crabmeat, removing any shells, and add to the soup. Stir gently in order to keep the crab pieces whole. Taste and adjust the seasonings.

Remove the soup from the heat and let it sit for at least 30 minutes to allow the flavors to blend. Heat gently when ready to serve.

Crawfish Bisque

The authentic version of crawfish bisque takes two days to make, boiling and peeling pounds of crawfish. It can be fun as a joint effort, but such a delicious dish deserves a shortcut that makes it available to busy cooks and those without an abundance of fresh crawfish.

MAKES 4 SERVINGS

3 tablespoons plus ½ cup vegetable oil, divided

2 pounds fresh crawfish tails, divided, or 2 frozen (1-pound) packages, thawed, divided

1 onion, chopped and divided

1 bunch green onions, chopped and divided

1 green bell pepper, chopped and divided

3 garlic cloves, minced and divided

¾ teaspoon salt, divided

¾ teaspoon freshly ground black pepper, divided

¾ teaspoon Creole seasoning, divided

2 cups bread crumbs, made in a food processor from stale French bread

1 egg, beaten

⅔ cup plus ½ cup all-purpose flour, divided

5 cups seafood stock or water

2 tablespoons tomato paste

Pinch cayenne pepper, or to taste

2 cups cooked long-grain white rice

2 tablespoons chopped flat-leaf parsley

Heat the oven to 350°. Spray a large baking sheet with nonstick cooking spray and set aside.

Heat 3 tablespoons of the oil in a large skillet and sauté half the onions, green onions, bell pepper, and garlic. Add 1 pound of the crawfish and sauté for 5 minutes. Remove the mixture to a food processor and grind to the consistency of ground meat. Transfer the mixture to a bowl and add ¼ teaspoon of the salt, ¼ teaspoon of the pepper, ¼ teaspoon of the Creole seasoning, the bread crumbs, and the egg and combine well.

Place ⅔ cup of the flour in a shallow baking dish. Roll the mixture into 1-inch balls. Roll the balls in the flour and place them on the baking sheet. Bake, turning the balls several times, until lightly browned all over, about 35 minutes. Set aside.

Heat the remaining oil in a medium, heavy pot over medium-high heat. Add the remaining flour, stirring constantly, until it turns a peanut butter color. Add the remaining onions, bell pepper, and garlic, and cook until translucent. Add the stock or water, tomato paste, the remaining salt, pepper, and Creole seasoning, and the cayenne pepper, and simmer, covered, for 15 minutes.

Mince the remaining crawfish tails and add to the bisque and continue cooking for 15 minutes. For a smooth bisque, blend with a hand blender. Add the crawfish balls and simmer for 5 more minutes.

Serve in bowls over the rice. Sprinkle with parsley.

Crawfish Étouffée

"Étouffée" means "to smother" in French. The dish is comparable to a stew, and in south Louisiana it usually contains crawfish. Peeled crawfish tails, fresh or frozen, are more widely available than ever, although we have a run on the market in Louisiana. Imported Asian crawfish are also available and at lower prices in many markets, but in Louisiana we prefer the local catch. Fat from the crawfish heads is an integral part of the dish, and most brands include it with the tails. This dish is best if left to sit for a while or refrigerated overnight before serving.

MAKES 8–10 SERVINGS OR ENOUGH FOR
A CROWD AT A PARTY BUFFET

- ¾ cup butter or vegetable oil
- ¾ cup all-purpose flour
- 1 large onion, chopped
- 1 bunch green onions, chopped, white and green parts separated
- 1 green bell pepper, chopped
- 3 celery stalks, chopped.
- 4 large garlic cloves, minced
- 3 tablespoons tomato paste
- 6 cups seafood stock or water (see Note)
- ½ teaspoon dried thyme
- 3 bay leaves
- 1 teaspoon Creole seasoning
- 1 teaspoon salt
- 1 tablespoon fresh lemon juice
- Cayenne pepper and freshly ground black pepper, to taste
- 2–3 pounds crawfish tails with fat
- 3 tablespoons chopped flat-leaf parsley
- Cooked long-grain white rice, for serving

In a large, heavy pot, melt the butter or heat the oil over medium heat. Add the flour and stir constantly. If using butter, cook the roux until it turns a blonde or golden color. If using oil, continue cooking, stirring, until the roux is medium brown. Add the onions, the white parts of the green onions, the bell peppers, the celery, and the garlic and sauté, stirring, until translucent.

Add the tomato paste, stock or water, thyme, bay leaves, Creole seasoning, salt, and lemon juice, season with the cayenne and pepper, and bring to a boil. Reduce the heat, cover, and simmer for 20 minutes, stirring occasionally and skimming any fat off the top. Add the crawfish, parsley, and green onion tops, bring to a boil, reduce the heat, and simmer for 10 minutes. Remove the bay leaves.

When ready to serve, reheat gently and serve over the rice.

NOTE ✳ If you happen to peel your own crawfish, you can boil the heads and peelings to make a stock. If you're using leftovers from a crawfish boil, reduce the cooking time after adding the crawfish to the étouffée. Packaged crawfish tails are not fully cooked.

Crawfish Pies

In respect to Hank Williams's famous song about Louisiana, "Jambalaya (On the Bayou)," crawfish pie is mandatory in a cookbook about gumbo and jambalaya. There are many styles, from bite-size appetizers to whole pies. This recipe makes small pies, the size of individual chicken pot pies, but the filling can be used in other configurations if desired.

MAKES 5 (5-INCH) INDIVIDUAL PIES

Enough dough for four 9-inch pies (store-bought is fine)

2 pounds crawfish tails with fat, divided

6 tablespoons butter

6 tablespoons all-purpose flour

2 medium onions, chopped

1 green bell pepper, chopped

4 garlic cloves, minced

2 cups half-and-half

4 tablespoons sherry

2 tablespoons fresh lemon juice

1 teaspoon salt

15 turns on a black pepper mill

1 teaspoon cayenne pepper

4 tablespoons chopped flat-leaf parsley

1 egg white, beaten

Preheat the oven to 350°.

Roll out the pie dough to ⅛-inch thickness. You should have enough dough for five 5-inch double-crusted pies. To get the right size for the bottom crusts, place one of the pans upside-down on the dough and cut the dough 1 inch from the edge of the pan. The top crusts should be cut at 5 inches for the best fit. Place the bottom crusts into the pie pans and keep the top crusts cold in the refrigerator.

In a food processor, chop half the crawfish tails until nearly ground. Leave the others whole.

Melt the butter in a medium, heavy pot or large skillet over medium heat. Add the flour and stir constantly until the roux is light brown. Add the onion and bell pepper and sauté for about 5 minutes. Add the garlic and sauté 1 minute more. Add the half-and-half, sherry, lemon juice, salt, pepper, cayenne, and parsley and cook for 5 minutes. Add the chopped and whole crawfish and cook 5 minutes more.

Fill each of the prepared pie shells with about 1 cup of the crawfish filling. Cover with the top crusts and crimp the edges. Cut several slits in the top crust and brush with the egg white. Place the pies on cookie sheets and bake until the filling is bubbly and the crusts are golden brown, about 1 hour.

Dirty Rice

Dirty rice is also called rice dressing and is served alongside a variety of meats, including turkey. Meat variations can include chicken gizzards, pork sausage, or smoked sausage. It is generally very spicy and especially good with fried chicken. It can also be used as a stuffing for poultry.

MAKES 8–10 SERVINGS

3 cups water

1½ cups long-grain white rice

¼ plus 1 teaspoon salt, divided

2 tablespoons vegetable oil

1 onion, chopped

6 green onions, chopped, white and green parts separated

1 green bell pepper, chopped

2 celery stalks, chopped

3 garlic cloves, minced

1 pound ground beef

1 pound chicken livers, chopped

½ teaspoon freshly ground black pepper

½ teaspoon cayenne pepper

⅓ cup chopped flat-leaf parsley

Bring the water to boil in a medium saucepan. Add the rice and ¼ teaspoon of the salt. Reduce the heat to low, cover, and cook until all the water has been absorbed, about 20 minutes.

In a medium, heavy pot, heat the oil and sauté the onion, the white parts of the green onions, the bell pepper, and the celery until translucent. Add the garlic and sauté a minute more. Add the ground beef and brown, stirring. Add the chicken livers and continue cooking and stirring until the beef and livers are cooked through, about 10 minutes. Add the pepper and cayenne, cover, and simmer for 5 minutes.

Stir in the parsley and green onion tops. Gently fold in the rice. Serve with Louisiana hot sauce on the side.

Eggs Sardou

Living in New Orleans offers many magic moments, about half of which involve food. One of my favorites is having brunch at one of the legendary New Orleans's restaurants. I like it best when dining al fresco and, occasionally, when a jazz trio is serenading me. On a picture-perfect day, there is nothing quite like sipping turtle soup (see recipe on page 110) and then enjoying Eggs Sardou on a brick patio under the oaks. The original Sardou recipe was invented at Antoine's in honor of French playwright Victorien Sardou, who dined there. This is a popular variation of that recipe, which included truffles and anchovies.

MAKES 4 SERVINGS

FOR THE HOLLANDAISE SAUCE

2 large egg yolks

1½ tablespoons fresh lemon juice

2 sticks unsalted butter

Salt and freshly ground black pepper, to taste

FOR THE EGGS

2 (9-ounce) bags fresh spinach

1 tablespoon olive oil

1 teaspoon minced garlic

⅓ cup heavy cream

Salt and freshly ground black pepper, to taste

8 fresh-cooked or canned artichoke bottoms

2 tablespoons white vinegar

8 eggs

To make the sauce, place the egg yolks and lemon juice in a blender. Pulse several times to mix.

Melt the butter in a glass pitcher in the microwave, being careful not to boil it. Gradually pour the butter into the egg mixture and blend until a thickened, creamy sauce forms. Season with salt and pepper.

To make the eggs, prepare the spinach by sautéing it in the olive oil in a saucepan, stirring, just until wilted and still bright green. Stir in the cream, season with salt and pepper, and keep warm.

Heat the artichoke bottoms and keep warm.

Fill a skillet or shallow pot with 2½ inches of water. Add the vinegar and heat to medium hot.

One at a time, crack 4 of the eggs into a small cup and gently pour them into the water. Simmer the eggs until they rise to the top of the liquid, and then turn them over with a spoon. Cook until the whites are set but the yolks are still runny. Remove with a slotted spoon and pat dry with paper towels. Repeat with the remaining eggs.

Spoon a serving of the spinach on each of 4 plates. Place 2 artichoke bottoms on each plate on top of the spinach and place an egg on each artichoke. Spoon the hollandaise sauce over all and serve immediately.

Grits and Grillades

Grillades was a favorite dish of the early Creoles, who often served it for breakfast or brunch. It is still a popular brunch dish for parade parties and for midnight country club parties after the Carnival balls. The common choice of meat is beef round for slow cooking. White veal round takes less time to cook and thus makes for a quicker meal.

MAKES 6 SERVINGS

---

1 (3-pound) beef or veal round steak, pounded to about
   $\frac{1}{4}$ inch thick
Salt and freshly ground black pepper, to taste
1 cup all-purpose flour
$\frac{3}{4}$ cup vegetable oil, divided
1 large onion, chopped
1 green bell pepper, chopped
1 bunch green onions, chopped, green and white parts
   separated
3 garlic cloves, minced
1 large tomato, chopped
1 tablespoon tomato paste
$\frac{1}{2}$ cup red wine
3 cups water
1 teaspoon red wine vinegar
$\frac{1}{2}$ teaspoon dried thyme
1 tablespoon Worcestershire sauce
Salt, freshly ground black pepper, and Creole seasoning,
   to taste
3 tablespoons chopped flat-leaf parsley
Grits to serve 6, cooked according to package directions

Cut the beef into roughly 2 × 3-inch pieces. Season both sides liberally with salt and pepper.

Heat ¼ cup of the oil in a large, heavy skillet and place the flour in a shallow bowl or plate. Dredge each piece of steak in the flour, shake off the excess, and brown on both sides. Transfer the meat to paper towels.

Add the remaining oil to the skillet and sauté the onions, the white parts of the green onions, the bell pepper, and the garlic until translucent. Add the tomato, tomato paste, wine, water, vinegar, thyme, Worcestershire sauce, and meat and season with salt, pepper, and Creole seasoning. Bring to a boil. Reduce the heat, cover, and simmer until the meat is tender, about 1½ hours. Add the parsley and green onion tops and serve over the grits.

Natchitoches Meat Pies

I take the easy way out on these pies and use refrigerated pie dough, but feel free to make your own piecrust. They are named for the town that made them famous, Natchitoches (NACK-ah-tish), Louisiana, which is where the movie Steel Magnolias *was filmed. Meat pies date back to the to the late 1700s, when they were made of beef and pork and served as street food. Today they are made with a variety of stuffing ingredients. Natchitoches is a kind of Creole outpost in the state's otherwise Anglo-Protestant Bible Belt. However, these pies are also popular farther south, especially at festivals such as New Orleans's Jazz Fest.*

MAKES ABOUT 24

2 tablespoons vegetable oil

1 large onion, chopped

6 green onions, chopped

1 green bell pepper, chopped

3 garlic cloves, minced

1 pound ground beef

1 pound ground pork

1 teaspoon Creole seasoning

$\frac{1}{2}$ teaspoon salt

$\frac{1}{2}$ teaspoon freshly ground black pepper

$\frac{1}{4}$ teaspoon cayenne pepper

$\frac{1}{4}$ cup all-purpose flour

1 package (2 crusts) refrigerated piecrusts

2 egg whites, beaten

In a large, heavy skillet, heat the oil. Add vegetables and sauté until translucent. Add the meat and cook, stirring occasionally, over high heat for a few minutes. Reduce the heat and continue to cook, chopping up the meat with a spoon, until it is thoroughly browned. Add the seasonings and flour and continue to cook for 10 minutes. Remove from the heat. The filling can be made ahead and refrigerated until you are ready to use it.

When you are ready to make the pies, preheat the oven to 350°. Spray 2 cookie sheets with nonstick cooking spray.

Place the refrigerated piecrusts on a flat surface and roll them out slightly thinner. Using a medium biscuit cutter, cut out circles. Place a heaping tablespoon of the filling on one half of each circle, leaving the edge clear. This will be the bottom of the pie. Fill a small bowl with water. Dip a finger in the water and wet the edge of the bottom half of the dough and fold the top over to form a turnover. Seal the edges together with the tines of a fork and place the pies about 1 inch apart on the prepared cookie sheets.

Brush the pies with egg whites and make a couple of small slits in the top of each pie. Bake until golden brown.

Oyster Artichoke Soup

Whether in a dip, soup, or side dish, oysters and artichokes are a match made in heaven. This quick and easy soup makes a great entrée with plenty of hot French bread. Be careful not to overcook the oysters or they'll get chewy. Serve with hot sauce on the side.

MAKES 6–8 SERVINGS

3 dozen shucked oysters with their liquor, plus extra liquor, if available

1 stick butter

½ cup all-purpose flour

1 large onion, chopped

6 green onions, chopped, white and green parts separated

2 celery stalks, chopped

4 large garlic cloves, minced

6 cups oyster liquor and seafood stock (or, in a pinch, chicken stock)

1 (14-ounce) can quartered artichoke hearts, drained and cut into bite-size pieces

¼ teaspoon cayenne pepper

1 teaspoon Creole seasoning

½ teaspoon celery salt

1 teaspoon Worcestershire sauce

Salt and freshly ground black pepper, to taste

1 cup half-and-half

2 tablespoons chopped flat-leaf parsley

Strain the oysters and reserve the liquor. Check the oysters for shell fragments and set aside.

In a heavy pot, melt the butter over low heat and add the flour, stirring constantly, until thick and just beginning to turn brown (a blonde roux). Add the onion, the white parts of the green onions, and the celery and sauté until wilted. Add the garlic and sauté another minute.

Add the oyster liquor, stock, artichokes, cayenne pepper, Creole seasoning, celery salt, and Worcestershire sauce and season with salt and pepper (start with just a small amount of salt since the oysters may be salty). Cover and simmer for 10 minutes. Add the half-and-half, bring almost to a boil, and add the oysters. Reduce the heat and simmer for several minutes or until the oysters curl. Turn off the heat and stir in the green onion tops and parsley. Adjust the seasonings before serving.

Oyster Dressing

In Louisiana, you don't have turkey without oyster dressing. In my family, we've always had two dressings on Thanksgiving and Christmas—oyster for the locals and cornbread for those who moved here from other parts of the South. Some cooks combine the two, but I prefer French bread for the oyster dressing. Oysters are in peak season around the holidays, so I think this is how it all started.

MAKES 8–10 SERVINGS

---

1 day-old loaf French bread, torn into bite-size pieces
(9 lightly packed cups)
3 dozen shucked oysters, strained and liquor reserved
Oyster liquor plus enough chicken or turkey stock to
make 2 cups
1 stick butter
1 onion, chopped
1 bunch green onions, chopped
3 celery stalks, chopped
3 garlic cloves, minced
3 tablespoons chopped flat-leaf parsley
½ teaspoon salt, or to taste
12 turns on a black pepper mill
½ teaspoon cayenne pepper, or to taste
1 teaspoon ground sage
2 eggs, beaten

Place the bread in a large bowl, cover with the stock, and let soak for 1 hour. Check the oysters and remove any shell fragments.

Preheat the oven to 350°. Melt the butter in a skillet and sauté the onions and celery until translucent. Add the garlic and sauté a minute more. Add the vegetables to the bread, along with the parsley, seasonings, and eggs. Mix well.

Spread the dressing in an 11 × 13-inch baking dish or 2 smaller ones and bake until puffy and golden brown on top, about 45 minutes.

Oyster Pot Pie

Most cooks call this oyster pie; I call it oyster pot pie because you serve it with a spoon like chicken pot pie. You can bake it in a pie plate or a casserole dish, and you can use a double crust or only a top crust. Either way, it is a delightful entrée for oyster lovers.

MAKES 6 SERVINGS

2 dozen large or 3 dozen small shucked oysters, with their liquor

1 cup sliced fresh mushrooms

1 tablespoon butter

4 tablespoons vegetable oil

4 tablespoons all-purpose flour

6 green onions, chopped, white and green parts separated

$\frac{1}{2}$ green bell pepper, chopped

1 celery stalk, chopped

2 large garlic cloves, minced

$\frac{1}{4}$ cup andouille sausage or smoked ham, chopped into $\frac{1}{4}$-inch pieces

1 teaspoon Creole seasoning

1 teaspoon Worcestershire sauce

2 dashes of Tabasco sauce

2 tablespoons chopped flat-leaf parsley

Salt and freshly ground black pepper, to taste

2 piecrusts, homemade or store-bought, refrigerated

1 egg white, beaten

Strain the oysters, and pour the liquor into a large measuring cup; add enough water to make 1 cup. Check the oysters for shell fragments and set aside.

Heat the butter in a small skillet and sauté the mushrooms until they are limp. Set aside.

In a large skillet or medium pot, heat the oil over high heat; add the flour and stir constantly until the roux starts to brown. Reduce the heat to medium and cook, stirring constantly, until the roux is the color of milk chocolate. Add the onions, the white parts of the green onions, the bell pepper, and the celery and cook until wilted. Add the garlic and cook a minute more. Add the oyster liquor, sausage or ham, Creole seasoning, Worcestershire sauce, and Tabasco sauce. Cover, reduce the heat to a simmer, and cook for 15 minutes.

Turn up the heat to medium-high and add the mushrooms and oysters. Cook until the oysters curl, about 4 minutes. Turn off the heat and stir in the green onion tops and parsley. Season with salt and pepper. Cool.

Heat the oven to 350°. Place one of the crusts in the pie plate. Add the oyster mixture and cover with the top crust, crimping the edges. Cut several slits in the top crust to release steam, and brush the crust with the egg white. Bake for 45 minutes or until the pastry is browned.

Oyster Rockefeller Soup

Oysters are one reason to live in south Louisiana. We use them in all ways imaginable. As if oysters Rockefeller were not decadent enough, someone invented oyster Rockefeller soup, an excellent way to enjoy this dish at home. To make the dish invented at Antoine's and said to be "as rich as Rockefeller," you must first buy a sack of oysters as it is illegal to sell them individually still in the shell. We buy them shelled by the dozen, pint, quart, or gallon for cooking and use them in many wonderful dishes. And, sometimes we go ahead and buy the 40-pound sack to eat them raw or cook them on the half-shell.

MAKES 6 SERVINGS

1 quart shucked oysters with their liquor, or 3 dozen oysters
    with 3–5 cups liquor
1 stick butter
½ cup all-purpose flour
1 bunch green onions, chopped
½ cup chopped green bell pepper
½ cup chopped celery
1 teaspoon minced garlic
1 (10-ounce) box frozen chopped spinach, thawed
¼ cup chopped fresh sweet basil
5 cups oyster liquor and/or seafood stock
2 tablespoons Herbsaint or Pernod
½ teaspoon Creole seasoning
Tabasco sauce, to taste
2 teaspoons Worcestershire sauce
White pepper, to taste
½ cup chopped flat-leaf parsley
1 cup half-and-half
Salt, to taste

Strain the oysters, reserving the liquor. Check the oysters and discard any shell. Set aside.

Melt the butter in a large, heavy pot. Add the flour and stir constantly over medium heat to make a blonde roux. Add the onions, bell pepper, and celery and sauté until translucent. Add the garlic, spinach, and basil and sauté a minute more. Add the oyster liquor and/or seafood stock gradually and stir until well-blended. Add the Herbsaint or Pernod, Creole seasoning, Tabasco sauce, and Worcestershire sauce and season with pepper. Cover, reduce the heat to low, and simmer for 15 minutes.

Taste and adjust the seasonings. Add salt at this point, if needed, depending on how salty the oysters are. Add the parsley, half-and-half, and oysters and simmer until the oysters curl, a minute or 2. Serve with plenty of hot French bread.

Redfish Court Bouillon

Any firm, white-fleshed fish can be used for this dish, which usually is cooked in a pot on top of the stove. My preference is to leave the fish whole and bake it in the oven with the sauce on top. It makes a lovely presentation. If you prefer, you can buy about two pounds of fillets instead of the whole fish, cut them into pieces, cook them in the sauce, and serve over rice.

MAKES 4–6 SERVINGS

1 (3- to 4-pound) firm, white-fleshed fish such as redfish or
    red snapper
3 tablespoons extra-virgin olive oil
1 medium onion, chopped
3 green onions, chopped
½ green bell pepper, chopped
1 celery stalk, chopped
3 garlic cloves, minced
1 large tomato, chopped
1 (15-ounce) can tomato sauce
Juice of 1 lemon
1 tablespoon Worcestershire sauce
¼ cup red wine
½ teaspoon dried thyme, or 2 teaspoons chopped fresh
½ teaspoon dried basil, or 2 teaspoons chopped fresh
½ teaspoon cayenne pepper
1 teaspoon sugar
Salt and freshly ground black pepper, to taste
2 tablespoons chopped flat-leaf parsley

Heat the oven to 350°. Remove any scales remaining on the fish and rinse well. Dry and place in a large baking dish with 2-inch sides. Refrigerate until the sauce is ready.

Heat the oil in a medium, heavy pot and sauté the onions, bell pepper, celery, and garlic until translucent. Add the tomatoes, tomato sauce, lemon juice, Worcestershire sauce, wine, thyme, basil, cayenne pepper, and sugar and season with salt and pepper. Bring to a boil, reduce the heat to low, and simmer, covered, for 30 minutes.

Add the parsley, taste, and adjust the seasonings.

Spread some of the sauce on the bottom of the baking pan. Sprinkle the fish with salt and pepper all over and place in the pan. Cover the fish with the sauce, placing some inside the body cavity. Bake, uncovered, for 30 minutes, or until the fish is just done at the center (using a knife, the flesh at the thickest part of the fish will easily pull away from the bone). Cover with foil and keep warm until serving.

Red Beans and Rice

Red beans and rice are served every Monday throughout New Orleans in restaurants and on home tables. The tradition began when homemakers did their wash on Mondays and wanted something on the stove that needed little attention. They cooked red and white (great northern) beans and dried lima beans. I use kidney beans here. The only other thing that has changed since then is that there is no particular laundry day in most homes.

MAKES 8–10 SERVINGS

1 pound dried kidney beans

2 tablespoons vegetable oil

1 large onion, chopped

1 bunch green onions, chopped, white and green parts
   separated

1 green bell pepper, chopped

2 celery stalks, chopped

4 garlic cloves, minced

6 cups water

3 bay leaves

$\frac{1}{2}$ teaspoon dried thyme

1 teaspoon Creole seasoning

1 ham bone with some ham on it, preferably, or 2 ham hocks
   or $\frac{1}{2}$ pound ham chunks

Salt and freshly ground black pepper, to taste

1 pound smoked sausage, cut into $\frac{1}{2}$-inch-thick rounds

2 tablespoons chopped flat-leaf parsley, plus more for serving

Cooked long-grain white rice, for serving

Place the beans in a large pot, cover with water, soak overnight, and drain.

In a large, heavy pot, heat the oil and sauté the onions, the white parts of the green onions, the bell pepper, the celery and the garlic.

In a large skillet, brown the sausage. Set aside.

To the pot add the beans, water, bay leaves, thyme, Creole seasoning, and ham and bring to a boil. Reduce the heat, cover, and simmer for 2 hours, stirring occasionally, adding the sausage 30 minutes before the cooking is complete.

Remove the bay leaves, stir in the parsley, and serve in bowls with the rice. Sprinkle bowls with more parsley, if desired.

Shrimp and Grits

New Orleans has adopted this South Carolina dish with such gusto that it is a regular in many restaurants and homes. The beauty of it is that it is not only delicious but quick and relatively easy to make for guests.

MAKES 6 SERVINGS

---

3 pounds large shrimp (about 15 to 20 to the pound),
    peeled and deveined
5 tablespoons butter, divided
8 green onions, chopped
5 large garlic cloves, minced
Zest and juice of 1 lemon
$\frac{1}{3}$ cup dry white wine
1 tablespoon Worcestershire sauce
1 teaspoon Italian seasoning
Freshly ground black pepper, to taste
$\frac{1}{2}$ teaspoon plus $\frac{1}{4}$ teaspoon salt, divided
1 teaspoon Creole seasoning
2 tablespoons chopped flat-leaf parsley
1 cup quick grits
$4\frac{1}{4}$ cups water
$\frac{1}{4}$ cup freshly grated Parmesan

Melt 4 tablespoons of the butter in a large, heavy skillet over medium heat. Add the onions and garlic and sauté until wilted. Add the shrimp and sauté, stirring, for a few minutes until they turn pink. Add the lemon zest and juice, wine, Worcestershire sauce, Italian seasoning, pepper, Creole seasoning, and ½ teaspoon of the salt and simmer for about 3 minutes. Do not overcook the shrimp. Remove from the heat and sprinkle with parsley.

To cook the grits, bring the water to a boil in a large saucepan and add the grits in a steady stream while stirring. Add the remaining salt. Cover, reduce the heat to low, and simmer for about 10 minutes. Remove from the heat and stir in the Parmesan and remaining butter. Serve the shrimp over the grits on plates or in bowls.

Shrimp Rémoulade

This classic French Creole dish is usually served over shredded lettuce. It can go on individual plates as an appetizer or on a platter with toothpicks for a party hors d'oeuvres. Horseradish and Creole mustard make it quite spicy. It is a favorite at old-line New Orleans restaurants as well as home parties.

MAKES 6–8 SERVINGS

½ cup chopped green onions
½ cup chopped celery
¼ cup chopped flat-leaf parsley
2 garlic cloves, minced
½ cup fresh horseradish (found in refrigerated section of
    grocery stores)
½ cup ketchup
¾ cup Creole mustard
2 tablespoons Worcestershire sauce
3 tablespoons fresh lemon juice
⅛ teaspoon cayenne pepper
Salt, freshly ground black pepper, and cayenne pepper,
    to taste
3 pounds large peeled and deveined shrimp
Shredded lettuce, about 4 cups

In a bowl, combine all the ingredients except the shrimp and lettuce and mix well. Taste and adjust the seasonings.

Several hours before serving, place the shrimp in a large bowl. Gradually stir in the sauce until the consistency is to your liking. Some may prefer all of the dressing and others, less. Serve over shredded lettuce.

Pepper Jelly

This popular home party recipe has been around for eons but never fails to please. Perhaps it's the local taste for spicy food that keeps it on the table. I like to make it for Christmas gifts, coloring it red or green.

MAKES 8–10 SMALL JARS

6–8 large jalapeño peppers, minced, to yield ½ cup
⅓ cup minced green bell peppers
6½ cups sugar
1½ cups red wine vinegar
1 (6-ounce) bottle Certo or 2 (3-ounce) packages
6 drops red or green food coloring

Remove the stems and seeds from the peppers and chop very fine or process in a food processor. Combine all the ingredients except the Certo in a medium saucepan and mix well. Bring to a boil, and boil for 2–3 minutes, stirring often. Remove from the heat and stir in the Certo. Pour in sterilized jelly jars and seal.

Serve over cream cheese for spreading on crackers.

Stuffed Mirlitons

In Louisiana, it's a mirliton. In the Southwest, it's called chayote. And these are just a couple of names for this widely available pale-green squash. The French version of this dish calls for shrimp and crabmeat. We add some Italian touches as well. You can find many a mirliton vine in the backyards of New Orleans homes.

MAKES 6–8 SERVINGS

(1–2 MIRLITON HALVES PER SERVING)

6 mirlitons

7 tablespoons butter, divided

1 medium onion, chopped

1 bunch (6–8) green onions, chopped, white and green parts separated

2 celery stalks, chopped

4 garlic cloves, minced

1 teaspoon Italian seasoning

1 teaspoon Tabasco sauce

1 tablespoon fresh lemon juice

Salt and freshly ground black pepper, to taste

2 pounds medium shrimp, peeled and deveined, or 1 pound peeled frozen shrimp, thawed

1 pound lump crabmeat

1¼ cups Italian bread crumbs, divided

In a large pot, boil the mirlitons whole until tender when stuck with a fork, about 1 hour. Drain and cool.

Meanwhile, melt 4 tablespoons of the butter in a large skillet. Add the onion, the white parts of the green onions, and the celery and sauté until transparent. Add the garlic and sauté a minute more. Add the seasonings and lemon juice and remove from the heat.

Cut the mirlitons in half lengthwise and remove the seeds. Scoop out the flesh, leaving a shell of about ¼-inch thickness. Add the mirliton flesh to the skillet and simmer for about 5 minutes. Stir in the shrimp and green onion tops and cook, stirring, until the shrimp turn pink. Mix in ½ cup Italian bread crumbs and crabmeat, tossing gently so that the crabmeat stays in chunks.

Line a greased baking sheet with mirliton shells. Stuff the shells with the seafood mixture and sprinkle each with 1 tablespoon of the remaining bread crumbs. Cut the remaining butter into small pieces and dot the tops of the mirlitons.

Bake until brown on top, about 30 minutes. Or brown under the broiler in the last few minutes of cooking. Serve immediately.

NOTE ❋ The stuffed mirlitons can be placed in freezer bags and frozen before baking for later use. Thaw before baking.

Turtle Soup

My husband and I once bought a large snapping turtle and set out to make turtle soup. Little did we know that turtles have hundreds of bones, and it took all day just to clean it. Now we know to buy frozen boneless turtle meat, which is available at some seafood markets in 2-pound packages. But we usually eat this heavenly Creole dish at Commander's Palace or Brennan's, where it is a menu staple.

MAKES 6 SERVINGS AS AN ENTRÉE,
12 SERVINGS AS AN APPETIZER

2 pounds boneless turtle meat, cut into 1-inch pieces
Salt and freshly ground black pepper, to taste
10 tablespoons butter, divided
5 cups water
2 medium onions
2 green bell peppers
3 celery stalks
6 large garlic cloves
$\frac{1}{2}$ cup all-purpose flour
$1\frac{1}{2}$ cups tomato sauce
1 teaspoon Creole seasoning
$\frac{1}{2}$ teaspoon dried thyme
$\frac{1}{2}$ teaspoon Italian seasoning
3 bay leaves
$\frac{1}{2}$ teaspoon salt
$\frac{1}{2}$ teaspoon freshly ground black pepper
2 tablespoons Worcestershire sauce
$\frac{1}{2}$ teaspoon Tabasco sauce
Juice of 1 lemon
$\frac{1}{2}$ cup good-quality sherry, plus additional for serving
4 cups chopped spinach
3 tablespoons chopped flat-leaf parsley
4 hard-boiled eggs, chopped

Sprinkle the meat lightly with salt and pepper.

Heat 2 tablespoons of the butter in a large, heavy pot and, in batches, brown the meat on all sides, removing one batch to a plate to brown the next.

Return all of the meat to the pot, cover with the water, and bring to a boil. Reduce the heat to low, cover, and simmer for about 1 hour, or until the meat is fork tender. Remove the meat to the plate and strain and reserve the stock.

When the meat is cool enough to handle, shred with your fingers and chop it into a fine dice. You may want to do this in the food processor. Set aside.

In a food processor, finely chop the onion, bell pepper, celery, and garlic. Set aside.

Rinse and dry the same pot you used to cook the turtle meat. Melt the remaining butter in the pot over low heat; add the flour and cook, stirring constantly, to make a roux the color of milk chocolate, about 10 minutes. Add the chopped vegetables and cook until very wilted. Add the tomato sauce and cook about 5 minutes. Add the stock, Creole seasoning, thyme, Italian seasoning, bay leaves, salt, pepper, Worcestershire sauce, Tabasco sauce, and lemon juice. Cook, covered, over medium-low heat for 30 minutes.

Add the sherry, spinach, and parsley and cook another 10 minutes. Remove the bay leaves and stir in the eggs.

Serve in bowls and pass extra sherry.

Index